MW00883450

The Incomplete Dudeist Priest's Handbook

By Reverend Gary M. Silvia

ABIDE UNIVERSITY PRESS
www.aui.me/press

Contents

Foreword 6

Introduction 8

What is Dudeism? 11

A Little About the Philosophy of Dudeism 11

Dudeism's Pyramid of Abiding 17

Dudeist Compeers 23

What Does it Mean to Abide? 34

What do Dudeists Do? 36

The Dudeist Practitioner 42

Rituals Celebrating Birth 45

Christening 46

Baptism 50

Solemnizing a Wedding 52

Preparing for the wedding 54

Performing the Wedding 55

Wedding Introduction 56

Wedding Ceremony 57

Wedding Conclusion 58

Sample Wedding Ceremony Scripts 59

Simple Wedding Script 59

Dudeified Wedding script 60

A Dudeified script that is a bit longer, with ring exchange.
.... 61

Checklist for Wedding Officiants 63

Funerals 65

Other Ceremonies 70

Priestly Dude-ties 74

Explaining Dudeism 74

Ministering to someone who is experiencing existential crisis. 77

Life Skills for the Dudeist 81

Get Ordained at The Church of the Latter-Day Dude 81

Meditation 82

How to Manage Money 86

Rolling a J 90

Mixing a White Russian 93

Cleaning a Pee-Stained Rug 95

Shitting in the Woods 97

Digging a Cathole 98

Digging a Latrine 99

Take it With You 100

Avoiding and Surviving a Bear Encounter 103

Finding a D&D Game 110

How to Take a Slacker Nap 113

Dudeist Prayers 115

The Dude's Prayer 115

The Calm Psalm 116

The Serendipity Prayer 117

Dudeist Affirmation 118

A Dudeist's Wish 118

The Dudely Vow 119

Conclusion 121

DEDICATION

I would like to dedicate this book to my friends and family who helped make me who I am today, especially my wife Heather, who has put up with me all these years. I also want to give special thanks to Oliver Benjamin, the Dudely Lama, not just for all his help editing and formatting this book, but also for being dudely enough to create Dudeism in the first place.

Foreword

I first met Gary in person in 2011 at a Lebowskifest in Lousiville, Kentucky. At that time, The Church of the Latter-Day Dude (Dudeism) was just getting off the ground and I was excited to help spread the word to some like-minded compeers at a Lebowskifest. Gary and I had enjoyed some online banter prior to that, but after finding out I would be hosting a Dudeism booth at the festival, he offered to drive all the way down from Maine and help out any way he could.

Anyone who has ever met Gary knows that when it comes to "help" he's like Santa's elves and the Beatles all rolled into one. With his cheerful enthusiasm, easygoing attitude, and wry sense of humor he helped make the weekend a huge success, especially considering I'd brought an Italian film crew in tow to do a documentary on Dudeism, and a comic book convention conveniently invited us to appear to flog our newly published *Abide Guide*. By the time it was over, Gary and I were good buddies.

Over the next couple of years, Gary became an ever-more instrumental part of Dudeism – contributing essays to *The Dudespaper*, interfacing Dudeism with Bernie Glassman's Zen Peacemakers (Bernie wrote The Dude and the Zen Master with Jeff Bridges), being interviewed for podcasts as a representative of the Church, and assorted other what-have-you.

Ultimately, Gary's involvement with Dudeism reached its logical next step – he was hired as the Church of the Latter-Day Dude's Minister of Public Relations in 2014 and has been my Right-Hand Dude ever since. Gary's dudely duties over the last decade have helped make Dudeism what it is today – still probably the world's slowest-growing religion, but surely one of its grooviest.

Now Gary has turned his talents towards a literary connection – producing this convenient handbook for Dudeist priests everywhere to enjoy. Encapsulating a wide variety of tips and topics, *The Incomplete Dudeist Priest's Handbook* is actually a lot like Gary himself – funny, philosophical and, well, really quite slender. This is not a weighty tome to wade through; it's a quick and convenient reference and reminder for those who walk (or shuffle) the Dudeist path.

Although we expect to expand this handbook as Dudeism itself expands, Gary has done the invaluable job of setting the ball in motion, and rolling one for the rest of us to pass around.

Proud we are of all of him.

Reverend Oliver Benjamin

The Dudely Lama of Dudeism
www.dudeism.com

Introduction

Have you ever mentioned to someone you are a Dudeist priest, and they responded by asking you what the hell you're blathering about? Or maybe someone got wind that you can preside over a wedding and now they want you to help them get hitched to their special lady friend? Or suppose a goon just peed on your rug, but you think, hey, how can I just clean this thing and avoid having to deal with millionaires and pornographers altogether?

Often serious and sometimes humorous, this handbook is here to aid the practicing Dudeist as they face these situations, and more.

This is *The Incomplete Dudeist Priest's Handbook*, a helpful field guide for Dudeist priests. This handbook is incomplete because no single document can ever cover all the different ways in which one can abide as a Dudeist. However, this handy handbook will give some answers, even as incomplete as they are, that may help the practicing Dudeist to function as abidingly as possible in this continuing human comedy. Herein you will find some explanation about the philosophy of Dudeism and what it means to abide, suggestions for arranging ritual ceremonies, and some useful life skills for the aspiring Dudeist priest.

This book begins with a discussion about the philosophy of Dudeism, while attempting to avoid creating dogmatic absolutes. It considers what Dudeism is and is not. We will create an abiding pyramid of physiological and psychological needs to help us better understand ourselves. Then we will take a brief look at other philosophies to help illuminate and better understand Dudeist philosophy. Finally tying it all together with a summary about what it means to abide and live a Dudeist lifestyle.

As Dudeism becomes more popular the call for Dudeist priests to perform weddings has increased. This handbook seeks to equip the practitioner with helpful advice as they go forth and do the Dude's work. We will discuss what duties a Dudeist minister may be expected to perform during their priestly career. We will also talk about common ceremonies that a Dudeist priest may be called upon to officiate, such as celebrating births and weddings, or providing comfort during times of loss.

We will wrap 'er all up with some instructions for performing basic life skills that may come up as you practice Dudeism. Featuring some key life skills that every Dudeist should be familiar with, like mixing a decent White Russian. Some of these life skills are likely to come in pretty handy, while others may be less likely to be needed but still good to know. We have even included how to avoid being eaten by a bear, just in case you're into the whole hiking and camping thing.

With this Incomplete Handbook in your pocket, you will be better prepared to answer you friends' questions about what it is you are blathering about. You will have the tools and important information for conducting ceremonies with a distinctly Dudeist flair. You will also have some life skills to help you as you abide in this world of ups and downs.

The Incomplete Dudeist Priest's Handbook is here to help you become a practicing Dudeist priest and fit right in there while sharing the wisdom of Dudeism and preforming far out rituals.

What is Dudeism?

The fundamental concept in Dudeism is to *abide*. That is the thread that ties this whole religion together. But what does it mean to abide? This section of *The Incomplete Dudeist Priest's Handbook* will attempt to answer that very question. The answer is simple but getting to the answer is a long road that we will traverse. We will have to answer many questions along the way. We will examine what Dudeism is and is not. We will discuss ways at looking at the philosophy of Dudeism. We will consider some other philosophies that may illuminate the philosophy of Dudeism. And finally, we will attempt to give the reader the best answer for what it means to abide.

A Little About the Philosophy of Dudeism

What is Dudeism?

The simplest answer is that it is a religion created by Oliver Benjamin in 2005 after he watched *The Big Lebowski*. While in Thailand, Oliver happened across the titular movie and began to examine some of the traits expressed by the Dude. Played by beloved actor Jeff Bridges, the Dude is the main character, a so-called slacker who is caught up in a neo-noir type mystery through a case of mistaken identity. The Dude's laid-back attitude and take it easy philosophy helps drive a comedy of errors as he is entangled with many other off-the-wall and sometimes aggressive characters. It was the Dude's attitude of acceptance, empathy, and good nature that Oliver homed in on.

Recognizing the Dude as an archetypal character that represented a worldview that was similar to, but different enough from, other philosophies, such as Taoism and Epicureanism, Oliver set about pulling the threads together into a cohesive idea about what a modern religion could look like. Thus, Dudeism was born.

Oliver was not alone in recognizing the subtle underlying philosophy within the Coen Brother's cult classic. Halfway around the world Zen Buddhist leader, Bernie Glassman, also saw something in the character of the Dude that led to him creating a slew of Buddhist koans based on the Dude's worldview. Jeff Bridges heard about Glassman's koans, and they became friends. Later, Bernie would become Jeff's Zen teacher, and they would write a book together, *The Dude and The Zen Master*.

We will not say that the Coen brothers intended any deeper philosophical implications to be plumbed from *The Big Lebowski*, but we also will not say that they did not. However, either through intent, happenstance, or blind luck they created a movie that would ultimately lead to the birth of Dudeism, and proud we are of them.

That is the technical answer to what Dudeism is. A religion based on a movie about a laid-back slacker interacting with the world and some rather uptight characters. "The Dude abides," Bridges' character states at the end of the movie, and that is what we are here to discuss. What does it mean to abide? It may be helpful to think about what Dudeism is not before we dive into what abiding is.

The Dude that can be named is not the eternal Dude

Firstly, Dudeism is just a word, a label used to describe a philosophy and the community that follows it. However, on a fundamental level it remains just a word, like the proverbial "finger pointing to the moon." Dudeism is simply a sign pointing toward a perspective, a perspective of abiding calm, one that is only knowable by the one perceiving it. Dudeism is experiential, all the words in the world spoken in all the possible combinations could never fully capture or contain what Dudeism means to the practitioner.

Dudeism is commonly referred to as a religion, *but is it though?* It depends on how one defines a religion. If the chosen definition of religion is that of a supportive community that has a shared worldview, one that is decorated with a founding myth, language, and rituals. Then sure, Dudeism is a religion, in that context. However, if the definition of a religion requires that it must have a deity or other paranormal explanation for the nature of existence, Dudeism doesn't fit the bill.

There is a glaring difference between Dudeism and most world religions. That difference lies in that while metaphysical claims that are common among other religions, Dudeism makes no such claims. Dudeism is a living worldview and practice. It concerns itself with this life, here, now, and as we find it. Dudeism makes no attempt to theorize about the creation of the world. Nor does it attribute phenomena to the existence of any god or gods. Dudeism does not preach about anyone's eternal soul. It's not that Dudeism denies any theories about creation or the existence of gods, just that it takes no stance on them.

Dudeism is not about trying to explain the unknowable. When it comes to the unanswerable questions that lie outside of our human senses, Dudeism remains silent. To questions such as: Where do we come from? What happens when we die? Is there a soul? Are ghosts haunting me? Where does the sock go when it disappears in the wash? Dudeism has the same answer to these and other mysteries. "Well, Dude, we just don't know." If the best minds in science cannot answer these questions the Dudeist would be well served to just kick back and abide that not-knowing.

Dudeism is not theistic, the important thing to remember is that Dudeism is a non-prophet, non-metaphysical religion. Within the Dudeist philosophy and worldview there are no revelations, no divinity to attribute any moral laws to, nor any theories regarding an afterlife.

In Dudeism there is no appeal to a cosmic entity, nor the following of a deeper plan concocted by a great designer. There is no notion of a sentient universe living out its will through us. When it comes to the seemingly universal question "what is the meaning of life?" In Dudeism, there is no answer, as far as we can see life has no intrinsic meaning.

Isn't that Nihilism? That must be exhausting

Not exactly. Just because a meaning for existence is not provided for us, it does not mean we cannot find or conceive of one for ourselves. Dudeism could be said to be inspired in part by the philosophy of *existentialism*, thus it is up to the individual Dudeist to create their own meaning for being. That said, Dudeism offers certain suggestions towards the creation of individual purpose. Perhaps it could be said that Dudeism is nihilism, but with several extra steps! If this all sounds absurd, it's because it is. Another close relative of Dudeism is *absurdism*, and we will take a closer look at absurdism later in this chapter. For now, it is important to not equate nihilism with Dudeism, even if they share some common aspects.

Dudeism is neither nihilistic nor theistic. For the Dudeist, life has no intrinsic meaning, but that does not make life meaningless. A Buddhist might recognize this as the so-called "middle path." When you sit and really think about it, existence is absurd! It cannot be, but here it is. Given this infinitely unknowable existence, it only makes sense to adopt or create the best ideas for living a joyful and abiding life. To do so cannot be any more absurd than it is to exist in the first place. The way in which we contrive rituals and meaning to apply to this existence not only defines our worldview, it helps us navigate the ins and outs of the whole durned human comedy.

Have you considered that, man?

We have discussed a bit about what Dudeism is not, so here we can begin to lay out some ideas about what Dudeism is: Dudeism is a worldview and a practice centered around the concept of abiding. It is a way of looking at the world and adjusting to the inescapable aspects of life. To abide is an open-ended affair. Dudeism helps one make the most of this experience of life by focusing on what is really important in order to find purpose and happiness.

Dudeism tries to identify what truly makes us happy, so that we can avoid the things that only make us think we are happy, but cost us more in suffering than they promise in joy. Dudeists value connections more than attachments, genuine friendships over possessive relations, celebration over escapism, and finding joy in the simple pleasures of rest and play.

Dudeism's Pyramid of Abiding

ABIDING ACTUALIZED
going with the flow
and feeeling groovy

IT'S A LEAGUE GAME
a sense of accomplishment and pride
just the right amount of acheivement

FRIENDS AND LOVERS
interpersonal relationships based on love and affection
either plutonic or zesty, we all want to be loved

SAFETY AND SECURITY
access to phisiological needs and
a private residence safe from nihilists

PHYSIOLOGICAL NEEDS
having food, shelter, and a few beers
the basics of ohysical survival

What do you need that for, Dude?

Epicurus reportedly once said "not what we have but what we enjoy, constitutes our abundance." Some consider Dudeism to be non-materialistic, and to a certain extent they are correct. In Dudeism it is about how we connect with the material world that brings us joy, not attachment or accumulation of material possessions. That said, there are some material things that we are unable to exist without.

In order to abide, we need to understand what material needs we have, and how they interact with our emotional and psychological needs. Abraham Maslow was an American psychologist who put forth a theory about what motivates humans. He proposed that human needs can be understood as a five-tiered pyramid.

Those familiar with Maslow's hierarchy of needs understand that we humans require certain material components before we can even talk about our philosophical needs. The five levels are: 1) physiological needs, 2) security needs, 3) the need for friendship and love, 4) the need to achieve some sense of self-esteem, and finally 5) self-actualization. He suggested that we tend to follow a particular order in achieving those needs, each level in turn becoming more crucial as the previous is fulfilled.

We can use Maslow's theory to construct our own "hierarchy of abidance" – a Dudeist pyramid of our own. Maslow has already done most of the work, but we can apply our Dudeist perspective and lay out a general set of needs to examine as we seek to abide.

Level 1: They are good burgers, dude

Physiological needs are those things that are required for life to sustain itself. Food, water, air, and few other creaturely needs are obvious to most. These are the things that would lead to our demise if not satisfied. No Dudeist will claim that we are being overly materialistic in seeking these things for survival.

This level of the abiding pyramid is easy to understand. A Dudeist must take care of their physiological needs first.

One cannot abide without food and shelter. Staying calm and still in that situation will lead to death.

Level 2: This is a private residence, man

Security is next in the hierarchy. Like the first level, this concerns existing versus not existing. We need to feel safe that nihilists will not be entering our private residences to threaten our johnsons, or worse. This can also mean having access to the previous material needs to sustain life. Are you employed, sir? There is no denying the anxiety people feel if they lose their job, thus losing their access to food and shelter. There are many ways of making a living, some that do not require making money, but make a living we all must.

It is when we satisfy the first two levels of biological needs that we can move on to the psychological ones and begin to seek friendship, achievement, and self-actualization. This is where Dudeism starts to have a lot to say on the matter. There is little need for Dudeism, or any philosophy, in the first two levels, as they are the closest to our primal drive for existence. There's little time to think about the meaning of life when you are drowning. A drowning Dude needs air – not philosophy or Lebowski quotes.

Level 3: She's my special lady friend

The need to connect with other humans on a deeper level emerges once we have some sense of our continued survival. Because what it is to live if life is lonely and unsatisfying? Love and friendship can be among the most rewarding pursuits for any Dude.

Dudeism encourages these sorts of connections, having a few friends is one of the most life affirming conditions. Having special lady or gentleman friends is also a natural and meaningful aspect of life. We all, for the most part, want to love and be loved. Whether that love is platonic or zesty, connection is crucial for our enjoyment of life.

However, sometimes our need for love can be clouded by attachment and possessiveness. Dudeism cautions that to engage in these sorts of relationships does not actually make us happier in the long run. Friends and lovers are not objects to be collected and controlled, they are co-conspirators in joy and abiding happiness.

Connection is sharing, attachment is possessing; connection asks, while attachment demands. Share with your friends, share your thoughts and feelings, share space, share experiences. Remember they are not yours to control, they are partners in creating the moments of our lives. Let them have their own sense of being beyond the connections you share, and tend to your personal space where they are not. The Dudeist should try to avoid attachment while also cherishing the connections they share with friends and lovers.

Level 4: See you at the finals

Once we feel safe and have love in our lives the need for esteem increases. Humans want to be noticed and lauded for their achievements. It is natural to want to earn the respect of others, and to respect ourselves. We can experience real joy from achieving a goal or gaining prestige from our compeers. Contrary to popular belief, Dudeism is not anti-achievement, yet it does caution against obsessive over-achievement.

Over-achievement is when one ignores the other fundamental needs outlined in this Dudeist version of the pyramid of needs. Seeking fame at the expense of maintaining fulfilling relationships or ignoring basic biological needs will leave the individual feeling worse in the long run. The rush of gaining higher status can be dampened quickly by loneliness and resentment of others. Working too hard to get there often causes us to neglect our relationships. Some may even skip sleep or avoid taking general care of their health. In these cases, the over-achiever has denied themselves true and lasting contentment in exchange for fleeting fame.

It is perfectly Dudeist to compete in the bowling tournament, but the experience shared with friends is the real prize. The Dudeist realizes it is all just play, and that getting so uptight that you would pull a gun on the lanes is contrary to the meaning of abiding.

Level 5: The Dude Abides

Through the Dudeist lens we can consider Maslow's self-actualization as abiding actualized. Attaining this state is among the highest of Dudeist ideals. It is the practice of Dudeist abiding in action, fully informing the practitioner in their daily lives.

When the Dudeist has achieved some mastery over the lower levels of this pyramid of abiding they have reached a point where they find it easy to accept themselves and reality for what they are. They tend to be spontaneous with their thoughts and actions, adjusting to life's ups and downs quickly with little anxiety. Their point of view is more objective and less self-centered.

The "self-abiding" Dudeist resists artificial social norms but does not aggressively push back against them. They are not at war with the culture they find themselves in – rather, they have simply transcended it. They see through the veils of conformity, trying to see things the way they truly are.

At the pinnacle of the pyramid the Dudeist finds creativity everywhere, and can see humor in many situations which might have otherwise got them down. They appreciate the many forms people and situations may take, remaining non-judgmental and open to all. Preferring to maintain friendships over material gains, the abiding Dudeist expects little from life, yet finds the experience deeply satisfying.

Since the abiding Dudeist has a firm sense of morality and ethics, they are also concerned with the welfare of others. They find joy in helping out where they can, and have a distaste for unnecessary aggression. Pacifism is a cornerstone of their philosophy, but they will not hide behind it if they can serve the greater good. Abiding is a calm, accepting, non-judgmental state. It is empathetic and kind, happy and aware.

Dudeist Compeers

At this point it may be helpful to consider some other philosophies that have similar perspectives to that of Dudeism. There are many concepts, ideals, and philosophies that exist in the world. Some are quite Dudely in their own right. Looking at a handful of similar philosophies can better illustrate what the Dudeist philosophy is all about.

For instance, many will point to Taoism as a compeer of Dudeism, at least when they are considering its original uncompromised first draft. Conversely, students of western philosophy may find many parallels between Dudeism and the teachings of Epicurus. Finally, a deeper look at Absurdism may help tie a few of the loose threads together.

Before we delve into the philosophies that follow, it is important to remember that this is an incomplete handbook. If we were to fully examine any of these philosophies to conclusion this would be a hefty tome, impossible to carry upon one's person. What follows is a set of brief essays meant to give a general understanding of their relation to Dudeism. We encourage the Dudeist practitioner to continue to familiarize themselves with these, and other philosophies, and investigate beyond the scope of this incomplete handbook.

Is that Some Sort of Eastern Thing?

There are more than a few people who consider Dudeism an updated form of Taoism's uncorrupted first draft.

Whereas Dudeism is founded upon wisdom derived from a movie, Taoism's foundation is the *Tao Te Ching*, an ancient document containing 81 verses. Loosely translated as "the Way of Virtue" the *Tao Te Ching* offers advice for perceiving the world, and how to act in accordance with it. A lot of people have seen *The Big Lebowski*, but surely many more than that have read the *Tao Te Ching*.

The *Tao Te Ching* is a collection of the teachings of Lao Tzu, who was said to be an incredibly wise man that lived in China around 500 BCE. Scholars debate the true authorship and timing of its first appearance, but that is more of an academic problem. For our purposes we can say Lao Tzu wrote the *Tao Te Ching*, and his inspired observations spawned Taoism as a religion.

In the 2,600 years of its existence, Taoism has been widely practiced in the East. It has also gone through some changes along the way, at some point someone thought that the power of a sorcerer could be derived from the Tao. Most Dudeists will agree that the addition of magical thinking did not improve the *Tao Te Ching*, but rather, did in fact corrupt it.

According to Lao Tzu, the Tao is the source of all things, manifest in the patterns and matter of reality. It is the underlying force that creates and binds the universe we find ourselves in. Wherever you look, whatever you think or feel, all the things and experiences in life are the Tao.

Lao Tzu saw that people can get lost in pursuit of the material things in this world and miss the deeper underlying truth of reality. He formulated that this misunderstanding of reality was detrimental to an individual's enjoyment of existence. What he saw was that people were fighting the flow of things, that they did not recognize the oneness of it all.

THE INCOMPLETE DUDEIST PRIEST'S HANDBOOK

Dudeism also looks at how the patterns of life are at work, and seeks to join with them, rather than fighting what is inevitable. There are things we do not like that happen, but in Taoism as in Dudeism we cannot always avoid them. The Dudeist accepts what is and tries to find one's place in the pattern, realizing that the material things in our world are just an expression of an underlying wholeness. In this way the Dudeist can enjoy them, without becoming attached to them.

"Go with the flow, man." This is the philosophy at the heart of Taoism, and likely why people make the connection to Dudeism. In Taoism *wu-wei* means effortless action. It is the art of doing nothing but leaving nothing undone. In Dudeism we say take it easy or go with the flow, but these are in a sense interchangeable with wu-wei. It means to act in accordance with the natural flow of things, without forcing them. To take it easy is to allow reality to unfold as it should, while being mindful to only do those things that arise spontaneously in an ethical and empathetic way.

Sometimes, there's a man

Epicurus was a man who lived around 300 BCE in ancient Greece, he sported a beard and had some groovy egalitarian ideas. He examined what makes us happy, and found that the answer was simple – one should literally live a simple life. He formed communes around his ideas of happiness eons before the first hippies rolled their first Js. A hedonist, he promoted doing what makes one happy, but only in ethical ways. To call him a hedonist in colloquial terms would be a misunderstanding, as his hedonism was grounded in virtue and simplicity. His was a philosophy of less is more – which led to less pain and suffering and more peace and happiness.

Known for his old-fashioned (for the time) beard, Epicurus and his philosophy were revolutionary compared to his contemporaries. He was known for arguing against some of the ideas within Platonism, and controversially opening his doors for all people to attend his schools, accepting people regardless of their gender or status in society. While other schools of philosophy would only allow elite and wealthy men, Epicurus welcomed the poor, slaves, and women to attend. This kind of egalitarianism was unheard of in Ancient Greece.

Epicurus sought answers to what it meant to live a good life. What he found was that to live a good life was to avoid pain and seek pleasure. It was a deceptively simple idea, one that becomes a bit more complicated when trying to discern what actually brings us either pain or joy. He posited that not all things we think of as pleasurable actually bring us joy in the long run. He saw that people with more stuff were not happier because they were always wanting more stuff or worried about losing the stuff they had. Whereas the people who had just a little more than enough stuff to make their lives easier tended to be far more tranquil and at peace. Epicureanism illustrates that the person in a modest safe dwelling eating good food can live a better life than a lonely overachiever eating a lavish feast in a mostly empty mansion.

Applying what he learned, Epicurus set up a community based on his philosophy, what today we might call a commune. This simple lifestyle became incredibly attractive to some. Soon communes based on Epicurus' teachings were popping up all around the Mediterranean. These communes flourished for hundreds of years, until they came into conflict with early Christianity. However, they were not totally obliterated – one form did persist into the modern era, the monastery. While far stricter and less open, monastic does have some things in common with Epicurus' communes.

The search for pleasure is a hedonistic pursuit that Epicurus saw as central to living a good life. To Epicurus life was not a dry run for some imagined afterlife. Adverse to the meta-physical ideas of his time Epicurus taught we should find happiness in the here and now, not in trying to win the favors of any god or gods through acts of virtue. However, he proposed that happiness cannot be attained through unethical thoughts or deeds. His ethical hedonism meant to look deeply into the effects of our beliefs and actions, to recognize that harmful behavior or animosity only leads to unhappiness for ourselves and others.

Epicurus wasn't throwing Jackie Treehorn-esque garden parties with half-naked women being tossed in the air. Epicurus was preaching about the simple pleasures in life that bring us true joy and satisfaction. He taught one of the most pleasurable things to have is friendship. He surrounded himself with friends, buying a large home (if one could afford it) but filling it with people instead of riches. This became the basis for his communes. Beyond friendship, Epicurus noted that although we thrive on meaningful work, we suffer under the materialistic drive that leads us to acquire more stuff. "Are you employed, sir?" Epicurus would probably respond "No time for that, I have too much work to do!" Epicurean hedonism is quite different from what we think hedonism is today – for example, sitting around drinking too much wine and having too much sex – it is about doing what is meaningful for us in the pursuit of *abiding* happiness.

Living an Epicurean lifestyle suits Dudeism to a T (or perhaps, a J). In a way, the film *The Big Lebowski* shows what happens when the Dude lets Walter talk him out of his Epicurean ways. The Dude already has friendship and a community. He seems to be able to afford the modest things he needs to survive and be hedonistically happy – such as having the fixings for White Russians, a J in his pocket, a few beers, and even the occasional trip to In-n-Out Burger. A pacifist, the Dude is kind and ethical, showing how to treat all people equally with dignity. It is only when he begins to attempt to get compensation and his rug back that his peaceful life of bowling and soaking in the bath gets interrupted. Ultimately, if he had let go of the rug, no matter how well it tied the room together, he would have experienced less suffering at the hands of millionaires, goons, and pornographers. By having one less rug, he could have enjoyed far more happiness and serenity. Then again, we would not have this marvelous movie to talk about and inspire us if that were the case.

I am the walrus

One must wonder if the character of Donny was in the movie just to remind us about the absurdity of the whole durn human comedy. When we seek meaning in this universe we are generally met with random and nonsensical answers. The rational philosopher can find no intrinsic meaning within the unfeeling universe driven by physics that resists conforming to the human need to find purpose in all things around us. It is absurd to look for answers that do not exist. This can be a dreadful state to find oneself in.

Absurdism had its nascent beginnings in the writings of Søren Kierkegaard during the existential movement of the nineteenth century. It was a time when philosophers wrestled with the idea of existential dread. Having rejected the meta-physical answers (like god and the afterlife), they searched for a replacement meaning for existence, but could not find one that made logical sense. Existentialism concluded that the search for meaning may actually be the answer to its own question. That was, until a French philosopher emerged on the scene shortly after WWII. Albert Camus taught that even the search for meaning is ultimately meaningless as well, as it is still subject to annihilation upon our death. Instead, he stated, we should embrace the absurdity of our condition and just live the life we have to its fullest.

Absurdism finds its place somewhere between nihilism and existentialism. The nihilist says life has no meaning, while the existentialist responds by saying we ourselves give life meaning. The absurdist, however, asks if both aren't true? The absurdist accepts the empty nature of being, then defiantly creates his own meaning to fill the void. He is fully aware that the meaning he creates is essentially as meaningless as existence itself, because that meaning is as transient as the person creating it.

Ride, abide, or die? That is the challenge absurdism puts to us. We can either ride with meta-physical answers given by some religions, abide by the meaninglessness of existence, or be so overwhelmed with dread that we take our own life. Absurdism considers anything other than abiding to be a form of suicide, either philosophical or physical. Philosophical suicide is when a person gives up and choses to accept the metaphysical ideas of others. In doing so, they surrender their gift of human freedom. To take one's own life in not the answer either, as it only reaffirms the meaninglessness of existence. Camus seemed to think that abiding the absurd is the only answer, and a heroic one at that.

It could be said that Dudeism is absurdism in action (or inaction, as in *wu wei*). A reason-based philosophy that ironically invites others to join in the acceptance of the absurd, Dudeism suggests ways to find one's own purpose through rational thought, creativity and pleasure. In short, Dudeism tries to offer the adherent a set of ideals and practices with which to find their own meaning in this nihilistic universe.

Two More for the Road

The world is full of religions and philosophies that have a bit to offer the contemplative Dudeist. This incomplete handbook can only take one so far into the vast world of philosophical ideas. There are interesting concepts to be found in many other philosophies such as naturalism, transcendentalism, and rationalism. Let us consider a couple more before we move on.

Here we take an even more incomplete look at two other philosophies worth mentioning: Buddhism and Stoicism. There is abundant inspiration for the Dudeist practitioner to take away from each of these philosophies.

The Duddha

Buddhism is one of the oldest religions to still be practiced, primarily in the East, it is also currently considered the fourth largest religion in the world. According to legend the Buddha, born Siddhartha Gautama, sat under a Bodhi tree and found enlightenment. His insight led to the Four Noble Truths, the central concept that ties Buddhism together.

The Buddha's Four Noble Truths are:

"There is suffering." Things are fucked here. Planes crash into mountains, and no matter what we do eventually even the Swiss watch stops ticking. The Buddha realized we are engaged in an inescapable struggle to keep the good in our lives, while avoiding as much of the bad as we can. Ultimately, however, we lose the struggle in an unsatisfying way.

"The cause of our suffering is attachment." Trying to resist reality and cling to things in our life is the source of our suffering. As we mourn the passing of a beautiful summer day, we create an unhealthy longing to bring it back instead of accepting the winter chill for what it is. In this way we try to hang on to the moments and things in our life regardless of their continued existence. Our grieving for what we perceive of as loss blinds us to moments we currently occupy. This condition leads to emotional pain that can negatively impact other aspects of life that we could otherwise be appreciative for in the moment.

"Avoiding attachments releases us from suffering." Let that shit go, man. Seemingly simple advice that we all have trouble putting into practice. It is all too easy to pine for what is lost or wish that party would go on forever. Unfortunately, human minds have difficulty accepting that which we feel makes us happy is impermanent, and that unhappy times are unavoidable.

"There is a path toward unattachment and release from suffering." You are in luck, you can find peace and acceptance with what is, just follow the path of the Dude, man. While the Buddhist may take this wisdom and walk their own Eightfold Path, we Dudeists have our own way to plod ahead which helps us remain chilled out while passing through the flames of suffering.

The Buddha's "just take it easy" vibe puts him right up there with other Great Dudes in History, we can all take comfort in that. If you're into the whole Eastern thing, we suggest checking out the teachings of the Buddha even further. There's a far out comparison of Dudeism and Buddhism at our very own Abide University here: www.aui.me/dudeism-and-buddhism

Mark it Zeno

A contemporary to Epicureanism is Stoicism. In fact they were even considered rivals – they argued like the Dude and Walter, despite the fact that they had so much in common with each other. Formed around 300 BCE by a merchant named Zeno of Citium, Stoicism's main point was that we can, and should, maintain our abiding chill regardless of what is happening to us. Basically, Stoics posit that it is not the problem that is the problem, but rather our reaction to the problem that causes us to suffer.

The Stoic seeks to live a virtuous life in accordance with nature and reason. They consider it their duty to pursue a dispassionate wisdom, since our emotions can lead us to act and think irrationally. They do not consider things such as illness or death to be inherently evil, rather just normal occurrences of existence that one can attempt to avoid through virtuous means, but not something to get hung up on when they cannot be avoided. For the Stoic, hedonistic pleasure is neither good nor bad in and of itself, however it should only be accepted if it conforms to an otherwise ethical way of life.

It is not hard to see the abiding wisdom of the Stoics, to ride with the ups and downs of life in a virtuous and wise way fits right in there with Dudeist philosophy. The

Roman Emperor Marcus Aurelius put this Dudely way of thinking into practice and is regarded as one of the few "good" rulers of ancient Rome. Stoicism is a school of thought that any Dudeist can benefit from a familiarity with, especially those who find themselves in leadership roles.

Philosophy is the backbone supporting Dudeist practice. We encourage all Dudeist priests to continue their learning about the world's philosophies far beyond where this incomplete handbook can take you. Go forth and contemplate!

What Does it Mean to Abide?

Equipped with the previous discussions in this section we can now weave all the loose threads into a functional idea about what abiding means in Dudeism. Like Dudeism, we know abiding is just a word, a representative of something larger than a string of letters. Our pyramid helps us ascertain what is important, both physically and emotionally, to achieving a state of abiding. Listening to Lao Tzu reminds us to watch for the flow of reality, so we can fit right in there. Epicurus suggests a lifestyle conducive to abiding ethically with friendship and joy. To abide is to embrace the absurd and seek individual meaning in the face of nihilism and the irrational.

Abiding is not about getting hung up on words such as Dude, Duder, or El Duderino. That's because simply naming something does not make it so. Abiding is a broad, multifaceted idea, not just a simple singular definition that can be easily tangled up in semantic arguments. This handbook uses a lot of words to try and explain what abiding is, but it is incumbent upon the reader to look past the prose and find the meaning within.

To abide is to take care of our physiological needs while we advance up the pyramid of our psychological needs. We abide through a careful examination of what we actually require while rejecting the things that unduly burden us. Understanding that not every materialistic drive will lead to happiness, the abiding individual avoids attachment while embracing connection with those things that truly supports them in their abiding.

Going with the flow is central to the concept of abiding. Lao Tzu advised heavily against fighting the way thigs are.

When we let go of our ideas of how things should be and begin to accept them as they are we are better able to operate within and through the patterns around us. The world is full of ups and downs, strikes and gutters. The Dudeist does not fight them, they abide them.

One way of looking at it is that to abide is simply to live, and to promote living. Abiding is a lifestyle focused on finding joy while avoiding suffering ourselves, and causing suffering in others. Sometimes that means less is more, as in having less stuff can give us more freedom to enjoy our lives. To this end, abiding is not possessive in its relationships, rather it seeks to foster friendships that give us joy without attachment. One does not need to join an Epicurean commune to start creating an abiding lifestyle of their own, although listening to the wisdom of a groovy bearded guy may help one abide.

Abiding accepts the absurdity of existence, it does not run to the irrational for comfort, but rather it creates its own meaning in defiance of an unfeeling universe. Abiding joyously strolls right past existential dread, choosing to see that the experience of life is itself enough to find purpose. Abiding tells oblivion to wait, we have things to enjoy, here, and now. The Dudeist stares into the abyss, flips it the bird, then turns around and gets back to living the abiding lifestyle.

To sum up, and put it in more Lebowskian phraseology: Abiding is a method and approach towards "taking 'er easy" and "fitting right in there" in the "whole durn human comedy" without "trying to scam anyone here." Far out.

What do Dudeists Do?

Dudeism is a practice, not a faith. So what does it mean to practice Dudeism? The answer is ever evolving and defined by the individual Dudeist. Understanding the philosophy of taking it easy is likely the only truly common aspect shared by the Dudeist community. Dudeism is not governed by any supernatural force, so it is on the individual and the community to co-create the practice of Dudeism.

There are several things that one can do to foster Dudeist abiding in their life. For example, Dudeists often dress for comfort, not for conforming. They tend to enjoy simpler pleasures in life. They seek friendships, even with people who do not share their world view. We can also take a few examples from the movie itself. For instance, Dudeist practice can involve play, meditation, quiet time, and various methods of keeping the mind limber.

That's my robe

We are all familiar with the fashion sense of the Dude. A Dudeist will tend to wear what makes them feel comfortable and authentically themselves. This does not mean you need to walk into the supermarket in your bathrobe, although you certainly can if you want to. Rather, Dudeism counsels that you should wear what feels right for you, free from society's expectations. If a three-piece suit feels right, go ahead and rock that style. It is about being true to your own nature, not what artificial demands others put on you.

Sometimes, what we wear can be subject to restrictions and levels of appropriateness. It can occasionally be an act of aggression to totally ignore some basic ideas of polite fashion. Be considerate of other people and situations as much as possible without betraying yourself. You can wear a bathrobe while going to the store, but perhaps not to a wedding or funeral.

A few beers

There is nothing in Dudeism that says one must imbibe to abide. That is a personal choice any Dudeist must make for themselves. Sometimes consuming a beer or cocktail can be an enjoyable experience. However, sometimes it can lead us away from abiding if we find ourselves too attached to alcohol. In which case it can be destructive to our lives and the lives of others.

If the careful beverage brings true happiness, far out. However, if it is harming you or those around you, you may want to reexamine whether it is truly adding to and enhancing your ability to abide. While the occasional drink may fall within our pyramid of abiding, it should not be crammed in there. Never insist that others join you for a beer if they do not want to. Everyone must abide in their own way.

Be reasonable in your choices regarding alcohol use. If it does not overpower or disrupt other aspects of your life, enjoy. If you find you do not like it, abstain. If it causes more troubles than joy, put it down, if you cannot put it down, seek help in overcoming addiction. Remember that our indulgences must enhance our lives, not detract from them.

A few friends

Friendship is one of the most important parts of an abiding life. The Dudeist values other people in their life. We take comfort in sharing with our friends, family, and lovers. Friendship is a source of great joy when maintained in a healthy and accepting way. Avoiding possessiveness while building on affectionate connections is prized among Dudeists and many others. The Dudeist chooses to decorate their lives with friendship in the same way the materialist decorates his or her home with fine art. Friends are cherished, but that does not mean it will be all smooth sailing.

As with everything, there can and will be ups and downs within any relationship. The Dudeist does not want close friends to deny their authentic selves in order to accommodate us. We also do not want to deny our authentic selves either. There are times when we disagree. The world is a large and complicated place, we cannot all be on the same thread always together. The Dudeist navigates the landscape of a relationship guided by the principles of Dudeism, focusing on the threads of love and affection that bind us to each other.

It's a league game

Play is important to all humans, not just the Dudeist. Recreation can invigorate us and bring us much joy. One does not have to join a bowling league, there are so many forms of recreation that are available. It can be a great adventure to find the ones that inspire you.

Everything can be play. For instance, although the Dude jokes about it in the film, golf can be enjoyable to the Dudeist. When all pretense is put away it is just a silly game of chasing the ball down a hole. In fact, all sports are! In that light, most games are a perfectly good excuse to wander around outside with friends. The Dudeist may even enjoy the competitive nature of games, so long as they do not take it too seriously. Friendly competition can be quite fun, when one focusses on the process of it all, and not so much on the winning. If someone becomes too attached to winning, they may end up pulling a gun (figuratively or literally) on the lanes. Keep your attention on the enjoyment of the game, not on winning or losing.

I'm going home

Spending some time in quiet solitude is another aspect of Dudeist life. Kick back lying on your rug with the sound of bowling playing if that is your thing. However you achieve it, a meditative state helps calm the mind, and allows us to focus better on what is truly important in our lives. Although we will propose some ways to meditate later in this handbook, here we consider *why* to meditate.

The purpose of meditation is to enhance the connection between body and mind, to find calming peace, and to help one be more present in their daily life. No matter what form meditation takes, it primarily seeks to help us quiet our thoughts so that we may hear our body. We may think we have arms and legs, but in mediation we want to feel them, as they are. When we inhabit our bodies in this way we can calm down and just enjoy the pure experience of existing. Being one with yourself, body and mind, can have a profoundly soothing effect. It can help us shake off the anxiety of constantly trying to perform and achieve in this hectic world.

Once you have shaken off the weight of existence through connecting the mind and body, you may start to recognize the more subtle feelings that lie within. In mediation we want to allow those feelings to arise naturally, without passing judgement. Greet each feeling with acceptance, allow yourself to feel what you feel without trying to define or interpret those feelings. What some call mindfulness, the Dudeist may call abiding. Either way, it is the attainment of this abiding state that is sought through meditation. It is why we meditate, to learn to better abide through practice.

Mind if I do a J?

It is no secret that many Dudeists are fond of the wonder plant we call cannabis. We certainly do not require Dudeists to engage in cannabis use, but we also do not discourage it in any way. Doing the occasional J is essentially a harmless and enjoyable experience. There may be cases where an individual may be less than rational in their cannabis use, but that is considerably rare. As the modern world matures and puts away archaic ideas of drug control, many people are accepting that cannabis use is a safe and life-affirming activity.

As with alcohol use, one must try to be rational with their indulgence. Right before taking a driving exam might not be the best time for a doobie. On the other hand, if you plan to weed the garden, maybe smoking weed will enhance the experience. Use intelligent abiding judgement for the appropriateness of cannabis use and nothing will be fucked here. If the time and place are groovy, go ahead, dude, we won't mind. One of the abiding principles of Dudeism is that if it doesn't hurt anyone else, and doesn't mess up your life, that's cool.

The Dudeist Practitioner

This is the modest charge we put before you

As a Dudeist priest, people may seek your services for certain rites and ceremonies. This section will lay out some commonly requested religious rituals, how to prepare for them, and some useful tips for performing services while also keeping it within the scope of Dudeist philosophy.

It is important to remember to act according to Dudeist philosophy, present yourself with abiding calm, and promote the fundamentals of Dudeism. This is to say: be cool, be chill, and do not be an asshole. People may have certain expectations about what a Dudeist priest may be like. They probably expect a pacifist who can roll with the ups and downs of life, one who can offer a bit of wisdom, and who embodies empathy in their work as a priest.

Applying the philosophy of Dudeism to your interactions, especially while conducting ceremonies is of utmost importance here. You can flub a line during a wedding ceremony, but you cannot pull a gun on the lanes (figuratively and certainly not literally), even if you see someone cross the line with a minor mistake. Be an example of abiding in your community, show that the wisdom of Dudeism is a path toward a more satisfying life.

Since we Dudeists do not have any official priestly vestiges, feel free to assemble appropriate attire for the occasion that you will be presiding over. You do not need to own a bathrobe or Pendleton sweater to be a practicing Dudeist priest. They don't hurt, but they are not required. We don't have any dress codes -- that must be exhausting.

When asked to perform any ceremony consider whether it conforms to basic Dudeist philosophy. Do not engage in any aggressive or illegal activities. No Dudeist would consecrate a dog fighting ring or bless an unhealthy relationship. Only perform those ceremonies that affirm the good things in life, or that bring comfort to those experiencing some of the downers that we all must accept. Ask first, does this lead to joy and/or comfort? Then proceed accordingly.

On a side note, in this section we end most ceremonies with "bar's over there." Do not get hung up on this. While it is fun, and can be informative when a bar is present, do not coerce people into drinking. This is a figurative closing for Dudeist ceremonies, not always a literal one. It may not be appropriate for certain audiences.

Finally, will this move you into a higher tax bracket? We at Dudeism neither require nor forbid the practitioner to charge for their services. A Dudeist priest may put in a lot of effort and time preparing for and conducting ceremonies. We hope do so out of a sense of purpose or other noble reasons. It is up to each individual practicing Dudeist priest to decide if it is appropriate for them to ask for compensation, and what that compensation might be. If you do charge for services, do your due diligence and check out the local costs of services in your area. Do not try to scam anyone.

Now that we have shared a little bit about how to approach being a Dudeist practitioner, here are some more concise instructions to help you on your path as a ceremonial Dudeist priest. Go forth and bring the abiding wisdom of Dudeism into the important moments of other people's lives. Stay true to Dudeism and yourself, and remember to have fun. Perhaps more than anything, this is what being a Dudeist is all about.

Rituals Celebrating Birth

Just helping her conceive, man

The perpetuation of this human comedy has been the cause for much celebration since time immemorial. Almost all cultures and religions have some rituals associated with the birth of a child. It is an important moment in at least three people's lives, and generally it is momentous to many more people than that. Welcoming the arrival of a new human to this plane of existence can be a joyous event, and rightly so. Few things are more worthy of celebration than the fruit of what is a natural and zesty affair. Humans have a fundamental drive to facilitate the continuation of the species, so the creation of new life is something we can all take comfort in.

Many people are familiar with the Christian rituals of christening and baptism. While similar and usually thought of together, there is a fundamental difference between the two. A baptism is a sacramental ritual where an individual, not necessarily an infant, is initiated into their faith. A christening is a ceremony for naming someone or something, often performed on infants, sometimes accompanying their baptism as well.

Clearly Dudeism is not a Christian sect, however those rites do not belong exclusively to Christianity. Various forms of initiation rituals and christenings occur outside of the Christian faith. Thus, there are also Dudeist baptisms and christenings, although they generally mean something rather different to the Dudeist.

We feel it is important to note that families can be formed with any arrangement of people who share a common thread of love and affection. They need not be the typical mother, father, and child. There can be two mothers or two fathers. The child could be the product of natural zesty endeavors by the parents or could be joining the family through an adoption process. So long as those involved share respect and love for each other, Dudeism is cool with any form a family takes.

There have been many rituals celebrating the arrival of new life that span time and culture. We do encourage the Dudeist practitioner to explore other cultural and historical rites as part of their preparations for conducting a ceremony celebrating the arrival of a new human. There are some groovy and far out ideas that have been part of current and historical birth rites. You may find some that would work well when added to any ritual you intend to perform.

Christening

Christening is pretty straightforward, and no, you won't be dunking the child into water and asking if they know where the money is. That is a baptism. Which we will discuss later.

A christening is a ceremony announcing the name of the little rug rat to the world in a formal and ritualistic manner. The ceremony can be short and to the point, or a grand formal affair – this is up to the parents. Talk with them to understand what they are looking for in a christening. There are no required aspects as far as Dudeism is concerned, this is a celebration of new life, not an excuse to proselytize.

Typically, a christening involves a newborn, but that does not have to be the case. For instance, a couple may be adopting a more mature child who already has a name. Do not let this throw you. Perhaps the child is taking on their new parents' last name. Whatever the case may be, the point is to celebrate the perpetuation of humanity. Far be it for us to get in the way of a good celebration or to complicate and muddy it up with dogmatic ideas so pervasive in other religions.

There are some important actions that should be part of the ceremony, discuss with the parents what proceedings they are comfortable with. Remember that christening in Dudeism is performative, not dogmatic.

Here is a typical arrangement for conducting a christening ceremony.

- The welcome: Acknowledge all those present and welcome them to the ceremony. This may be just the parents, or a large group of guests and participants in the exercise. Some parents may want a small private affair. Some may want a grandiose gathering of friends and family, if they are into that sort of thing.
- State the reason you are all there. Let everyone present know that the purpose of this ceremony is to officially bestow a name and possibly welcome the newborn to this durned human comedy.
- This is a good time for an optional reading from the Abide Guide, Dude de Ching, or other appropriate and inspiring written work. While far from required, this part can really jazz up the proceedings. Be thoughtful but have fun with it.
- Invite the parents to step forward and present the child.
- Ask the parents what name they have chosen for their child.

- Ask for a declaration from the parents that they are there to have their child christened. Ask them if they are committed to taking care of this child and intend to give it love and security. You can optionally ask if they intend to raise their child according to Dudeist philosophy. be sure to have discussed this last part beforehand, do not spring this on unsuspecting new parents – they have enough to worry about.
- If the parents have elected to have godparents, this is the part where you ask them to step forward and announce their intention to take on that role. Be sure to have had a conversation with the potential godparents beforehand.
- Conclude the ceremony by welcoming the baby to the world and announce the newborn's given name to those gathered for the ritual. Be creative, but the important part is making sure you do proclaim the child's name, that is what everyone is there for.
- Thank everyone for attending and point out where the bar is.

Here is a potential script to help you out. You can follow this script or use it as inspiration for creating your own.

Officiant: I welcome you all to this formal christening/naming ceremony. Dudes, we have gathered here to celebrate the arrival a new person to this human comedy. We, the new parents, and I, think it is far out that you have chosen to join us in this joyous occasion. Today we will bestow upon this child a name and introduce them to you and the world.

Optional Reading

Officiant: Would (parent) and (parent) please step forward with the child? What have you chosen as a name for this child?

Parents' response.

Officiant: Do you affirm that it is your intent to care for (child's name), to provide both creature and emotional comforts to (child's name)? To cherish them and protect them to the best of your ability? In front of these witnesses assembled here today, do you promise to uphold these commitments?

Parents' response.

Optional, godparents.

Officiant: Have you chosen godparents to step in and care for (child's name) in the event that you are no longer able to?

Parents' response.

Officiant: Would (godparents) please step forward? In the event that (parents) are unable to fulfill their commitment, do you affirm your intent to provide both creature and emotional comforts to (child's name)? To cherish them and protect them to the best of your ability? In front of these witnesses assembled here today, do you promise to uphold these commitments?

Godparents' response.

Officiant: Groovy.

Optional reading or statement.

Officiant: Dudes, it is my pleasure to now introduce (child's name) to you. May they enjoy all the benefits of a loving family, may their bond with (parents) grow and be a source of affection and security for all their life. We celebrate this family union. May it stand the test of time. The bar's over there.

Baptism

Baptism, well that is a bit stickier. A baptism generally refers to indoctrinating a person into a religious order. In Christianity, the person is often baptized with water, either anointed with holy water or dunked in a tub or body of water. Dudeism does not proselytize, and we certainly do not want to make philosophical choices for children. However, if someone choses to celebrate their child becoming a Dudeist, who are we to get in the way of a good party.

As a practicing Dudeist priest you may be asked to give a few words at such an event, and that's cool. The church has not set any rules to follow here. Potentially, if many people want a Dudeist baptism ceremony it may inspire us to lay out a more complete framework at some point in the future. For the time being, you the Dudeist practitioner, are on the front line. Your experiences here may lead to a more fleshed-out idea of what a baptism within Dudeism could look like.

Here are a few tips for conducting a Dudeist baptismal ceremony.

- Welcome everyone and announce the purpose of the ceremony.
- Talk a little about what Dudeism is and what it means to you.

- Invite the person being baptized to step forward and announce their intention to take on the Dudeist worldview.
- Say a few words welcoming them into Dudeism.
- Finish by thanking everyone for attending.
- Remind everyone where the bar is.

Keep it simple and fun, the last thing we want is to be taken too seriously at this time of baptism, as it has less to do with increasing our ranks, and more to do with having an excuse to get together and celebrate.

Solemnizing a Wedding

Does this place look like I'm married?

As a Dudeist priest you may be called upon to officiate weddings from time to time. Thousands of Dudeists have already obliged in conducting ceremonial duties for hopeful couples looking to wed. We have put together the following information to help our fellow Dudeists in their officiating duties. However, unlike some religions, we have no explicit "rules" concerning the performance of weddings, other than to keep it legal and harmless. Here are some things to consider as you prepare to officiate a Dudeist wedding.

First, let us look at what marriage means in the modern world. In legal terms marriage is essentially a contract between consenting adults for the purpose of forming a family unit, with all the benefits, conditions, and responsibilities that are required under the law. Humans also experience the primal desire to physically and emotionally bond based on attraction and affection. This may include the urge to procreate, but that is not necessary in forming romantic bonds and marriage. Marriage is about special friends and perpetuating the whole durned human race. People chose to marry to form a loving relationship based on affection and the accordant natural zesty enterprises which generally follow.

For some, there is a spiritual aspect to marriage. This differs greatly from one philosophy to another, but on some level, a sense of spirituality plays some part in making a lifelong commitment. It is important to take the opinions and beliefs of the parties being married into account and design the ceremony accordingly. As Dudeist wedding officiants we must keep an open mind and work with the couple getting married to honor their understanding of what that means.

Dudeism is gender-blind when it comes to all things. A Dude is a Dude, regardless of how they identify their gender or orientation. Naturally, this also applies to solemnizing unions, so if you are uncomfortable performing same sex weddings you may want to go back and examine Dudeist philosophy again. Wherever such marriages are legal, we Dudeists should be happy to wed any people who are there of their own free will and share a love and respect for each other.

As Dudeists we are not here to judge, but there are times when a Dude should not perform a marriage. For instance, one of the parties is not there of their own free will, as in they are being coerced or is underage and too young to marry. It is important that both people love and respect each other in order for us Dudeists to truly sanction such an arrangement. It must be a consensual and legal marriage formed through affection before a Dude should proceed to bind a couple in marriage.

The legality of a marriage is determined by the country and/or the state that the wedding takes place in. Always check with the local county clerk for verification about what is legal and required. Often you will need to file to be a registered officiant. It is also common that there be at least two witnesses to any wedding. Make sure you understand the laws where the wedding is to take place.

Preparing for the wedding

Make sure your important papers are in order. This usually means having a certificate of ordination and a letter of good standing from the governing body of the church. Laws vary from place to place but these documents are generally required. Check with the clerk's office where the wedding is to be performed to see what documents are required to register or be recognized as a wedding officiant. Make note of the process for registering the marriage after the wedding has been performed. The clerk's office must record the union for it to become legal.

If you have not already done so, you need to ordain with the Church of Latter-Day Dude here: https://dudeism.com/ordination. If required you can order copies of your certificate of ordination with seal, and letter of good standing here: https://dudeism.com/store/.

Sometimes the clerk's offices may require more documentation. Contact The Church of Latter-Day Dude at gary@dudeism.com subject: weddings, for any necessary documents not readily available in our online store.

Talk to the couple being married, discuss the ceremony with them, and find out what they are looking for in a wedding. Draw inspiration from them and their plans as you consider any readings or statements you want to make. There are sample Dudeist wedding ceremonies described later, but make sure to plan the wedding around the couple. Make it special for them on their special day.

Write out or print the wedding script on cards or a piece of paper. We have provided samples of wedding scripts you can follow or use to write your own. Pay attention to the parts of the ceremony that make the marriage legal. Usually, there has to be a formal affirmation by the parties involved stating their intent to wed. For extra visual effect, you might put the script in a binder, perhaps with a Dudefish sticker on the outside.

Practice, practice, practice. After you have taken care of the paperwork and talked to the couple, plan out the ceremony and practice it before the day comes. This is your chance to get a feel for your own voice and how the rhythm of the ceremony might go. Record yourself reading it out loud so you can hear what you sound like. Take care to work out any tripping points in the plan. Practice will help keep the ceremony from crashing into the mountain on the wedding day.

Performing the Wedding

Generally wedding ceremonies can be broken down into three distinct parts: an introduction, the ceremony, and the conclusion. These can be further broken down into different elements, and these elements can be arranged in whatever manner the officiant and couple to be married see fit. Beyond satisfying the law, a wedding ceremony can take nearly any form, from a simple declaration to an extravagant event. Weddings can be spiritual and deeply religious or entirely secular with no hint of religion at all. What is important is the declaration and celebration of the union being formed. That is what a wedding ceremony is all about: announcing to the world the couple's intent, and celebrating the occasion.

Here are some examples of the different parts that are involved in a wedding ceremony. This is just a suggested arrangement for the wedding event, so roll with any reasonable requests from the couple getting hitched.

Wedding Introduction

- **THE PROCESSION** - This is the part of the ceremony when the music plays, and the participants move to their final places for the actual ceremony. Traditionally this is when *Here Comes the Bride* will be playing as she and her procession make their way to the altar. Maybe this is something the couple wants to include in their wedding plans, maybe not. As the officiant it is your job to communicate with the couple being married to find out what their wishes are. This is completely optional, no need for a procession other than for the fun and spectacle of it all.

- **THE GREETING** - This is when the officiant, the Dudeist priest in this case, welcomes the attendees and announces the impending marriage. State who is getting married and a basic outline of the events to come. Even with the simplest of ceremonies some form of greeting should be included.

- **OPENING REMARKS** - This is where the individual creativity of the officiant comes into play, this is your chance to share some Dudeist philosophy regarding love and marriage. Make it your own but make it tailored to the wishes of the couple as well as the setting where the wedding is being performed. While optional, it is recommended to say at least a few words about the couple and their intent to wed, it really ties the ceremony together.

- **READINGS -** A good time to break out The Abide Guide, Dude De Ching, or any other inspirational reading you feel would be appropriate to the situation.

Wedding Ceremony

- **ADDRESS THE COUPLE -** Begin by speaking directly to the couple getting married, explain to them the gravity of the commitment being made. You can also address the those in attendance, explain to them why they are there. While not necessary, this is traditionally when the officiant or priest would ask "if anyone has reason why these two should not wed?"

- **VOWS -** This is one of the most important parts, and legally required under most circumstances, this is the Declaration of Intent. Traditionally the "I take this man/woman" and "I do" part of the wedding. Some form of formal declaration from each party getting married is generally required. This is not optional.

- **RING EXCHANGE -** The couple may choose to exchange rings or gifts as symbols of their love and the union they are forming together.

- **CANDLE LIGHTING -** Some couples like to ceremonially light candles in honor of their new union. This option can give a spiritual vibe to even a secular wedding. Candle lighting would certainly be welcome at any Dudeist service, perhaps with whale songs playing while the lighting occurs.

- **THE KISS** - This is what everyone came for, let the tension build a little, but do not hold out, let them have their first kiss as a married couple.

Wedding Conclusion

- **Closing Remarks** - Another chance for you the officiant to blather on about marriage, love, the couple, children, laws regarding the keeping of marsupials within city limits, whatever.

- **Introduction of the Newlywed Couple** - This is one of the steps that should be included, even if the ceremony is a simple one. This is the formal introduction of the newly formed union to the attendees and the world.

- **Recessional/Reception** - Once the newly married couple has been introduced it is time to celebrate the new union, so get off the stage and join party.

- **After The Wedding** - "Is this your homework Larry?" Make sure to get everyone's signature on any important documents. You do not want to find out later that one of the witnesses has kidnapped themselves and cannot be found to give their signature. Remember to file all the important papers with the clerk's office. The marriage is not legal until you have taken care of this part of the process.

Sample Wedding Ceremony Scripts

Here are some weddings scripts to aid you in your officiating duties. They are complete and ready to follow, or you can use them as inspiration for your own. Be prepared to make any adjustments that may be required by law.

When describing the parties involved, we sometimes use terms such as husband or wife in these scripts. As Dudeists we should not be uptight concerning the genders of those we are officiating for. Use the terms that are appropriate and satisfy both the local law and the wishes of the couple being married.

Simple Wedding Script

Here is a really simplified wedding ceremony, truly barebones stuff, and basically anything less is probably not legal.

The officiant opens the ceremony.

Officiant: Dudes, we are gathered here today to unite (first party) and (second party) in wedded matrimony. And that's cool, that's cool.

The officiant addresses the first party.

Officiant: Do you take (second party) to be your lawfully wedded wife/husband? If so, please answer I do.

After the first party declares their intent the officiant addresses the second party.

Officiant: Do you take (first party) to be your lawfully wedded husband/wife? If so, please answer I do.

After both parties have formally declared their intent to marry, the officiant solemnizes the marriage.

Officiant: By the authority vested in me by the Church of the Latter-Day Dude and the state of (state where the wedding is taking place), I now pronounce you (Husband or Wife) and (Husband or Wife).

Dudeified Wedding script

This script takes a little more liberty in length and added Dudeist sentiment. It's still very bare bones. You'd want to add a lot more to it.

Officiant: Dudely beloved, we have gathered here today to tangle the threads of (first party) and (second party) as they begin to weave the rug of marriage that will tie their lives together.

Optional reading or statement by the officiant or member of the wedding party.

The officiant addresses the first party.

Officiant: Dude, do you take (Second party) to be your lawfully wedded (wife/husband)? To be your special (lady/gentleman) friend, to hold in abiding matrimony, and not treat each other like objects? If so, please answer I do.

After the (first party) declares their intent.

Officiant: Far out!

Officiant addresses the second party.

Officiant: Dude, do you take (first party) to be your lawfully wedded (wife/husband)? To be your special (lady/gentleman) friend, to hold in abiding matrimony, and not treat each other like objects? If so, please answer I do.

Officiant: Far out!

After both parties have formally declared their intent to marry, the officiant solemnizes the marriage.

Officiant: By the authority vested in me by The Church of Latter-Day Dude, a stranger, and the state of (state where the wedding is taking place), I now pronounce you (Husband/Wife) and (Husband/Wife). Dude and Dude, you may now seal it with a kiss, or what have you. Let there be much cheer on this groovy day! Bar's over there.

A Dudeified script that is a bit longer, with ring exchange.

Opening the ceremony.

Officiant: Dudely beloved, we have gathered here today to tangle the threads of (first party) and (second party) as they begin to weave a marriage together. Few things are happier than celebrating the union of two Dudes looking to tie the matrimonial knot. Let the love (first party) and (second party) share with each other lead to many years of happiness and zesty affection. May their union be the rug that really ties together their love and affection.

Optional reading or statement by the officiant or member of the wedding party.

The officiant addresses the first party.

Officiant: Dude, do you take (Second party) to be your lawfully wedded (wife/husband)? To be your special (lady/gentleman) friend, to hold in abiding matrimony, and to not treat each other like objects? Do you promise to love and cherish them all the days as you abide this human comedy? If so, please answer I do, man.

After the (first party) declares their intent.

Officiant: Far out!

Officiant addresses the second party.

Officiant: Dude, do you take (second party) to be your lawfully wedded (wife/husband)? To be your special (lady/gentleman) friend, to hold in abiding matrimony, and to not treat each other like objects? Do you promise to love and cherish them all the days as you abide this human comedy? If so, please answer I do, man.

After the (second party) declares their intent.

Officiant: Far out!

The ring exchange.

Officiant to the first party: Do you have the ringer, man?

After the first party's response.

Officiant: Cool. As you place the ring on (second party)'s hand, repeat after me.

"With this here ring I promise to love you, to cherish you, and to hold you through the ups and downs of life. "

Officiant to the first party: Do you have the ringer, man?

After the second party's response.

Officiant: Cool. As you place the ring on (first party)'s hand, repeat after me.

"With this here ring I promise to love you, to cherish you, and to hold you through the ups and downs of life. "

After both parties have formally declared their intent and exchanged rings, the officiant solemnizes the marriage.

Officiant: By the authority vested in me by The Church of Latter-Day Dude, a stranger, and the state of (state where the wedding is taking place), I now pronounce you (husband/wife) and (husband/wife). Dude and Dude, you may now seal it with a kiss, or what have you.

Closing

Officiant: Ladies and gentlemen, we thank you for attending and sharing with us this joyous and groovy occasion. It is truly a wonderful thing to see love affirmed on this day. It is now my pleasure to introduce to you (first party) and (second party) as (husband/wife) and (husband/wife). Join me in offering them cheers. Bar's over there.

Checklist for Wedding Officiants

Here is a handy checklist to help you cover your bases. Refer to it as often as needed while you plan to officiate a Dudetastic wedding. Remember, it is up to you to satisfy the law, the people getting married, and to bring abiding chill to the wedding ceremony.

Before the wedding takes place

- Discuss the wedding with the couple and make your plan.
- Check with city/town clerk's office for full requirements for wedding officiants.
- Certificate of ordination or a letter of good standing is generally required. You may need special version is some areas.
- Write your own ceremony, use one of ours, or utilize any other appropriate script.

The wedding ceremony

- Introduce the ceremony.
- Have the couple make a declaration of intent, the vows.
- Conclude by introducing the newly married couple to the world.

After the wedding

- Gather the necessary signatures, the couple, you, and two witnesses.
- Complete the rest of the required paperwork.
- File the important papers with the city/town clerk's office.
- Party, this is one of the happiest times for friends to get together for some laughs and a few beers, do what you can to make it a joyous and safe time for all.

Whelp, that about covers weddings, Dude, go forth and help some folks get hitched.

Funerals

It may come to be that a Dudeist priest will be asked to conduct a funerary ceremony. This would be the least happy of all possible Dudeist ceremonies. In a life full of ups and downs, the death of a loved one may be the most profound and deepest downer there is. Meet it with grace and empathy, take time to consider the depth of suffering that follows in the wake of an individual's passing.

You should only agree to conduct a funerary service if you feel you can do so. Unlike other possible Dudeist ceremonies a funeral service would be the most serious. Much can be forgiven while conducting a wedding, a dropped line or pratfall may get a few harmless laughs. However, a funeral is not a time for levity, if you do not think you are prepared to deliver the type of service a funeral deserves we caution you to not take on such a task.

This is a terribly difficult time for those left behind after the death of their loved one. Listen to them with compassion and offer your condolences. Learn in what way they hope your service will give them comfort. Each situation will be different, but you can refer to this section for guidance as you prepare for the ceremony.

Life is precious but fragile, it can be snuffed out in many ways, some more devasting than others. A Dudeist practitioner should consider the manner of death. Sudden tragic deaths, particularly for those that are still young, can be especially devasting to friends and family. Sometimes death follows a long period of suffering with medical conditions, leaving a sense of relief as well as loss. Approach each instance in its own light, and tailor your remarks accordingly.

What follows is a potential outline of a funerary service. However, it is merely a suggested path. Let your intuition and compassion guide you. Not every part of this procedure may be appropriate to the situation, so this is not the time to get hung up on the rules. If you come from a place of understanding and good intent, you will not be over the line.

You may not be the only priest asked to speak at the funeral, in fact you should expect that there may be priests of different religious orders involved. It may be that you are supplemental as a Dudeist priest, playing second fiddle to another religious practitioner. Do not let your ego get in the way if this is the case. For many, Dudeism is supplemental to another religious denomination. Always respect their other religious beliefs.

Begin preparing before the day of the ceremony. Find out as much as you can about how the family would like that day to unfold. You will need to discover the crucial information to plan your part of the service. Meet with those who survive the deceased ahead of time. Introduce yourself and discuss how a Dudeism-inspired ceremony might go. Find out what their wishes are and what they feel is important to include in the service.

Familiarize yourself with the friends and family of the departed, learn about the person who is being remembered. It may be pertinent to learn of the circumstance of their passing. More importantly, learn about how they lived, what they enjoyed, what were their passions, and how they affected those around them. You can ask for stories and anecdotes from their friends and family, these can be included in the ceremony, or used to get a better understanding about who deceased was in life.

Inquire about how the family wishes the ceremony to be conducted. Will there be a funeral home involved, a grave side memorial, or both? Learn about what their expectations are for you. Ask if there will be other ministers involved. Ask if any family or friends would like to give a eulogy or other statement during the ceremony.

Talk with the funeral home director. Learn what their typical methods are for conducting services. Familiarize yourself with the people and the place where the funeral is to be conducted. The funeral home staff are there to help the proceedings go smooth and respectfully.

If you are the chosen minister to lead the service at a funeral home, there are typically three parts to the proceedings: The viewing, sometimes with an open casket; the ceremony, this is when the priest speaks to the family and those in attendance; and the recessional, which is how the ceremony concludes, often including the body being moved to the burial site.

Be present for the viewing. The viewing may include an open or closed casket, or possibly a picture board or other such reminder of the person being laid to rest. Generally, the priest will be standing by the coffin to greet and comfort those that spend this time to get their last look at the deceased. Be kind, listen and offer well wishes as appropriate. This may happen before or after the ceremony, or both. Be flexible, this is not about you.

Begin the service by asking the audience to stand as the family takes their seats at the front of the seating area. This is to show respect and honor their loss. Introduce yourself and the ceremony, explain why everyone has gathered on this somber day. Be sure to acknowledge the deceased and the bereaved.

Take a moment to perform a reading, recite a comforting poem, share a bit of Dudeist wisdom, or tell a story that is important to the family. Sometimes there will be music played or even a hymn sung. You should be aware of this and its timing from earlier conversations with the family and funeral home staff.

Conclude the service by thanking everyone for coming, let them know they brought comfort to the family and share some kind thoughts. Finish by informing everyone if there is to be anything else that follows, such as a wake or grave side memorial.

The recessional ends the service much the same way it began. There may be another viewing as people leave, again the minister would generally be standing by the coffin offering comfort and kind words. Often the recessional will continue with the casket being moved to the burial site. If it is in a different location, there will be a procession of people following the hearse in their cars. The priest sometimes rides with the family, but it is okay to meet them there after taking your own ride.

If you are part of the graveside service, the same basic steps apply with a little deviation. The minister leading the service, be it you or someone else, stands by the grave and waits for everyone to arrive and be seated. Once everyone is there and settled, welcome them to the service. Perform a reading or other short statement. Allow other ministers or those associated with the deceased to speak as well. After everyone has had the chance to speak, say a short comforting statement, and thank everyone for coming. In this instance, maybe leave out reminding everyone where the bar is.

We will leave you with a short list of tips to help you along.

- Prepare ahead of time, meet with the family, and assemble any readings you will include.
- Be present for any viewing, be prepared to offer kind words and wisdom to the bereaved.
- Open the ceremony by thanking everyone for coming.
- Talk about the deceased and share part of their story. Be mindful of the family's wishes and hopes going forward.
- Give a reading or short statement. You can share some philosophical wisdom of your own, just make it empathetic and appropriate.
- Allow others to speak, either planned or if someone has something they need to say in that moment.
- Conclude the service with another short statement and thank everyone for attending.
- Be present if there is another viewing.
- Be prepared to join a procession heading to the burial site.
- Follow the same basic introduction, ceremony, and conclusion steps for conducting the grave side service.

Those are the basics for preparing and conducting funeral service. If you decide you are up to the task, we suggest you do your homework, Larry! As stated previously, this is an incomplete handbook, we recommend you research funeral rites from other sources to better prepare.

Other Ceremonies

The big three milestones of life, birth, marriage, and death are not the only moments worth celebrating or honoring. A Dudeist practitioner may be called upon to perform many other rites, some more common than others. The number of reasons to celebrate and mark an occasion are limited only by people's imagination. If you are asked to perform any ritual or ceremony in the official capacity of a practicing Dudeist priest, there are a few things to consider before you agree: Is it legal? This should go without saying but do no bring down any heat on yourself or the church. Is it ethical? Do not be out there causing harm in the name of Dudeism, no one digs that. Is it within the purview of Dudeism? This is a little tougher to discern, but use your best judgement, contact the church if you have any questions. Once you have assessed the legality, ethics, and whether it is really a Dudeist thing, then begin to plan the ceremony.

Communicating with those asking for your services is the first step. Talk with them about what they expect and what you can do. Determine if it is a joyous or somber occasion. Sometimes it can be a mixture of the two, such as a retirement party. Is it going to be a formal affair, or a laid-back festivity? Knowing the wishes of those involved and the mood of the occasion will inform your next steps in getting ready for the big event.

Lay out the order of events based on your conversations with those requesting the service. Be mindful of what it is you are celebrating or solemnizing. Do not write a bunch of joke lines if it is a serious circumstance. Do not be too up tight if it is a cheerful party-like celebration. This is where your judgement and understanding of Dudeist philosophy comes into play.

If you have read through the other functions in this section, you have likely noticed a certain pattern to the flow of most ceremonies. There are typically three parts to the ceremony: the introduction, the ritual, and the conclusion. The introduction is when everyone is welcomed, and an announcement is made about why the ceremony is taking place. The ritual is the actual ceremony. The event then ends with a conclusion, some closing remarks and people are thanked for attending. There can be readings, music, or other statements interspersed within the ceremony – these add to the overall celebratory or solemness of the occasion. Remember to discuss your plans with the interested parties beforehand.

The introduction involves recognizing the people taking part in the ceremony and the audience in attendance. Keep it simple and warm. You are just saying hi to everyone in the room in a more formal way. After the welcome be sure to inform everyone why they are there. Let them know what the occasion is all about. Give them a preview of the activities to come and explain the importance of any ritual included. Optionally follow this part with a short reading or statement that illustrates the gravity of the ceremony. There may be music to be played in lieu of a reading – it depends on what the wishes are of those that requested the service.

Perform the rites or declaration of the ceremony. For instance, this would be the part of a wedding that asks the wedding couple to say their vows. This is generally the most important part, the whole reason everyone is there. Be as professional as the occasion calls for in conducting this part of the proceedings. There may be another optional reading or other statement here.

Finally conclude with some remarks about how the service has tied it all together. You can add some words about why this was an important moment for those in attendance. Review the meaning of the ceremony, then thank everyone for attending. If appropriate, remind everyone where the bar, or the reception is.

With these tips in mind, you should be able to perform a satisfying and uplifting Dudeist celebration or observance. Since this is an incomplete handbook, you will want to consult other sources other than this as you prepare your agenda. As a practicing Dudeist priest you should present yourself as well-rounded and considerate. Take on this task with grace and with an understanding of the principles of abidingness.

Things to remember. This simplified order of events involved in Dudeist ceremony is a quick reference for you as you are doing the Dude's work.

- Communicate with those you are going to perform a service for.
- Plan ahead, do not be like a child wandering into the middle of a movie.
- Always welcome participants and guests to the ceremony.
- Announce the purpose of the service, tell everyone why you are all there.
- Preform the service with confidence supported by your preplanning.
- Include other elements as appropriate, readings, music, or a song may add meaning to the ceremony.

- Conclude the ceremony and thank everyone for attending.
- Relax, and show people where they might get a drink.

Priestly Dude-ties

Being a practicing Dudeist priest may sometimes involve more than performing weddings or the occasional christening. People may seek your intuition and advice as a minister of Dudeism. If you are known to be a Dudeist practitioner, some people may approach you to enquire about the philosophy of Dudeism. Those that are interested will probably ask how they can be a chill Dudeist such as yourself. Then there may also be some that are searching for real answers to life's hardest questions in moments of existential crisis.

This part of *The Incomplete Dudeist Priest's Handbook* is here to help you engage with others in your capacity as a Dudeist priest. Here you will find some helpful advice for when you are discussing Dudeism with those just hearing about it the first time, or those looking to join our little beach community. This section will also seek to prepare you for interacting with people in need of wisdom to help them cope with the downers of life.

Explaining Dudeism

Dudeism, what's that? Many a Dudeist has been asked this question and they have come up with some creative and enlightening answers. Here are some thoughts and topics you can use while trying to explain what it is we are blathering about.

Give them a frame of reference. The best place to start explaining Dudeism is to make sure they are aware of the movie. You can ask if they are familiar with *The Big Lebowski*. Most people are, but if you run across someone who has not seen or heard of the movie be prepared to give a brief summary. Touch on the key points in the film that you find important to understanding Dudeism.

Once you have told someone that Dudeism is based on a movie they may give you some funny looks. Explain how the movie is just a founding myth, not to be taken literally. Unlike some other religions we know our founding myth is a fiction. But like all myths, it serves to inspire a deeper understanding about what it means to abide. It may not literally be true, but it holds a lot of literal truth.

One thing we learn from the movie is that the Dude had a good life, and it was only when he pursued compensation for his rug that he stepped out of his abiding ways. The Dude's rug brought him joy, but his attachment to it brought more suffering than it was ultimately worth. Explain that life is about more than the things we acquire and keep, and more about the experiences we have and the connections we make, even if they're impermanent. By the end of the film the Dude regains his Zen-like posture and remembers to abide.

Take the listener beyond the movie and begin to lay out the ideas behind Dudeism that can lead to a better life. In Dudeism the goal is to attain an abiding attitude toward life's ups and downs, to cherish the good and accept the bad, managing both with understanding and grace.

In Dudeism we focus on the things that bring us happiness, while avoiding things that cause suffering. We take care to sort out the two through self-awareness and careful examination of their effect on us both physically and emotionally. In this way Dudeism is hedonistic, but it is not devoid of ethics.

Dudeism is an ethical, pacifistic religion. It avoids unnecessary acts of aggression. It is kind and supportive. It will attend a friend's dance recital to support them, it will come to the aid of the helpless, it will listen to the plights of others, and it will try not to bum anyone out unnecessarily. Dudeism seeks to limit all harm, even if the one being harmed is a human paraquat that tried to ensnare us in a scam. When a Dudeist is called to action they do so with empathy and compassion. The Dudeist understands that life can be tricky, and not everything will turn out the way we want. While trying to do no harm, Dudeism goes with the flow.

You can add that Dudeism counsels non-judgmental acceptance of the way reality is manifest. It goes along with the good and bad of life without getting lost in the currents of emotion or attachment. Ultimately, we have no control over the course of life's events, and at times it can all seem meaningless, but there is a way of looking at it that creates a sense of meaning for the individual. Embracing the absurd, Dudeism's answer to oblivion is to find purpose and happiness in the now.

If they are interested in your blathering about Dudeism, direct them to the main website, www.dudeism.com for further information and possible ordination.

Some key points to cover while discussing Dudeism:

- Dudeism is a non-prophet religion, there are no divine revelations, and we do not have a Dudeist god to worship. Dudeism is a rational worldview that does not rely on any metaphysical claims to promote its philosophy of abiding.
- Dudeism is largely inspired by a movie, but it is not a fan club. In fact, one does not even need to see the movie to take on the Dudeist abiding

philosophy. Also, Dudeism incorporates much more than the movie: many religions, philosophies, books and even other movies.

- Dudeism does not proselytize: we are not aggressively trying to gather converts. If someone digs our style, great. However, it is not our intent to force Dudeism on anyone.
- Dudeism follows in the existential/absurdist traditions. In our view life has no intrinsic meaning, but we are free to apply meaning to existence, and that's cool.
- Dudeism avoids causing harm. Always concerned with ethics and the greater good, the Dudeist just wants everyone to have a positive experience of life – even nihilists.
- Dudeism leans into non-materialism but does not require any vows of poverty. It is okay to have money and things, so long as we avoid attachment to those things, and we see their true cost and benefits on our lives.

Hopefully, this will aid you in your conversations with those unfamiliar with Dudeism. Be patient and do not take offense if they are not picking up what you are putting down. People must come freely to Dudeism, we are not here to spring the Dudeist inquisition on anyone.

Ministering to someone who is experiencing existential crisis.

Once more, this is an incomplete handbook, meant only to help you begin to navigate these issues. There is little worry in talking about the wisdom of the Dude to the merely curious, but if someone is in major crisis you should refer them to professional help. Dudeism does not, and will never, proselytize. Do not risk someone's health and wellbeing while attempting to make Dudeism "their answer for everything." That is not our gig. We Dudeist priests are here to help people and not cause them any harm. Be considerate and rational in any situation where someone is experiencing any sort of emotional or psychological crisis. If it is beyond your modest abilities or qualifications, point them toward professional help. We will include some resources at the end of this section.

An existential crisis can occur for many reasons. It generally happens when we question our purpose for existence and what it all means. When our beliefs are challenged by loss or a major change in our lives, we may feel a sense of existential dread. The sense that life has lost its meaning can be rather uncomfortable, even leading to suicidal thoughts.

When someone comes to you with feelings of meaninglessness or existential dread, first listen to them. Acknowledge what they are experiencing without passing judgement, let them know their fears are valid. Then in a non-critical way suggest that there are other ways to look at the absurdity of existence that are life-affirming. In Dudeism we create meaning by looking at what makes us happy and gives purpose to our lives.

Ask them to think about the things they are grateful for. You can suggest they start writing down what makes them happy and lends purpose to their lives. Tell them it may help if they take some time to examine those things deeply, to see their true value in their life. Perhaps they are most grateful for the people in their lives. Suggest that strengthening or adding connections to other people may give them a sense of belonging.

Often existential crisis arises from the loss of someone close in a person's life. Help them accept the fact of the loss but remind them they can still form close friendships and love other people. You might tell them to reach out to those already in their life such as friends and family. Or you might suggest they look for ways to meet and connect with others. Maybe they have a hobby that can foster friendly connections with others or provides some feelings of joy and purpose in their private life.

Sometimes play or a hobby is a good way for people to spend their energy and create a sense of meaning in their life. It is not a bad idea to tell the person experiencing existential crisis to focus a little more on their hobbies. The moments we spend engaged in play with others is joyous and uplifting. Of course, there are solitary hobbies as well, and those quiet moments spent engaged in a task that brings us happiness can go a long way to providing a sense of mental wellbeing. Tasks can give us a sense of purpose.

If the person asking about the meaning of it all in this meaningless existence has a career that they find satisfying, point out that they already have a reason to be here. In fact, losing a job may be the spark that touched off someone's existential crisis. Tell those who are without purpose because they are out of work that they now have the time and space to consider what about their job gave them satisfaction, and to pursue that above other lesser considerations. Or perhaps they can focus on the other aspects of life that still give them joy while they seek balance.

Remind them that there is more to life than work, or friends, or even play. In Dudeism we seek to balance the parts of our lives to achieve a rounded approach that keeps us afloat when one aspect may be out of whack. Advise those going through existential crisis to consider how they have arranged the pieces of their life. Is there something out of balance that they can adjust to bring them a sense meaning and purpose?

Some people will respond to the advice we have laid out above, we all have moments of existential crisis that we need to learn to abide. Other times the sense of dread is too great, and a friendly philosophical discussion will not bring solace. As a Dudeist priest try to recognize the difference between a casual conversation about the meaning of life, the universe, and everything, and the person who is suffering depression and needs professional therapy. If someone is experiencing depression or anxiety help them find counseling. If the person is feeling suicidal and may act on those feelings direct them to help immediately.

Here is a short list of resources in the United States that you can share with a person suffering from depression, anxiety, or suicidal thoughts. As a practicing Dudeist you should familiarize yourself with these and more. For Dudeist Priests in other countries, similar resources should be available online.

> SAMHSA Treatment Locator Another source for referrals to low cost, mental health providers (800-662-4357)
> The National Domestic Violence Hotline provides 24/7 crisis intervention, safety planning and information on domestic violence (800-799-7233)
> The American Foundation for Suicide Prevention for referrals to support groups, mental health professionals, and suicide prevention (888-333-2377)
>
> The Suicide Prevention Lifeline connects callers to trained crisis counselors (800-273-8255)

Life Skills for the Dudeist

This section of the handbook is dedicated to some basic life skills we feel the practicing Dudeist might want to be acquainted with. Every Dudeist should know how to meditate and offer condolences. And even for those who don't partake, rolling a J and mixing a White Russian can be useful abilities to have. You may never need to worry about some of these life skills, but if goons break into your residence and soil your rug, or should you find yourself needing to poop while hiking, this section can come in rather handy. While not a final authority on these life skills, we offer them to you humbly, may they serve you well in your daily lives.

Get Ordained at
The Church of the Latter-Day Dude

Somehow you have reached this part of the handbook and are still not ordained in the church? Who knows, maybe you bought this book out of curiosity or to find out what your Dudeist friend has been blathering on about. Now, you are hip to the whole Dudeist thing and want to join us in our little beach community. We are here to help.

Ordaining in The Church of the Latter-Day Dude is free and easy. Simply go to www.dudeism.com and follow the links to the ordination page. Fill in your information and click the affirmation button. That's it, you are now a Dudeist priest!

Meditation

The practice of mediation dates back thousands of years. Thought to have originated within Buddhism, mediation has spread far and wide since the time of the Buddha. Many religions have some form of meditation, and Dudeism is certainly one. The reason mediation has been around so long and adopted by so many is that it really does work. The practice of mediation can help a person better understand themselves and the world around them. People who regularly meditate often feel a sense of presence that is peaceful and conducive towards leading an abiding life.

Most people are familiar with the image of the monk sitting quietly in the lotus position, in deep mediation, perhaps fingering some form of prayer beads. However, it doesn't have to be like that. Meditation can also be a dude lying on his rug and listening to the ambient sounds of bowling. Even free-form balance and stretching exercises can be considered meditation if they are performed in the right state of mind – the Dude even managed to do this with a White Russian in hand. There are many ways to meditate.

While form may affect the quality of one's meditation, especially in the beginning, mediation is about a state of being, not posture. Here we will describe basic meditation in the form of sitting meditation. We will then look at how one might incorporate what they learn into other forms of meditation.

For the beginner it may be helpful to start with the basics, sitting and breathing. Find a comfortable spot where you can sit for an extended period. This is usually done while cross-legged on the floor. However, if that position causes pain or discomfort then sitting in a chair is perfectly fine. In Asia, most people find it easy to sit in the cross-legged position, but for Westerners it can be unnaturally painful. Try to sit up as straight as possible with your hands in your lap or by your side. Take a few moments to feel your body in that position. Once you have found the position that suits you, relax your muscles, let all that tension go, man. Now it is time to focus on your breath.

Move your attention to the rhythm of your breathing. Feel the air flow into your body and follow it as it departs. Allow your mind to engage fully with your breath, let it become one with the body's movement, sense the rising and falling of your chest. You can think to yourself "in," as the air enters you, and "out," as it leaves you. This becomes a sort of mantra that will help you clear your mind of everything except your breathing. Stay in this moment as well as you can, for as long as you can, while meditating.

Thoughts will arise as you try to focus on your breath, your mind will want to remind you that it is already the tenth, and the rent is due. Along with thoughts, emotional feelings may emerge as well. We are not meditating to fight these thoughts and feelings. Rather, we should allow then to manifest. Meet them with non-judgmental acceptance, forgive your own thoughts and feelings, and let then slip away as easily as they arrived. If you find you are starting to be dragged away by your train of thought, refocus on your breathing. Do not consider these internal intrusions as some sort of failure, this is precisely why we meditate. In meditating, we learn to abide, to allow what is to unfold as it should.

You can set a timer beforehand. For beginners five or ten minutes may be enough to get started with the practice.

Over time you may want to extend the length of your meditation sessions. Everyone has their own idea of how much meditation is enough. People also have ideas about the way they can meditate beyond sitting like a monk. Let us now look at a couple of ideas for attaining the meditative state while not seated.

Once you have a good grasp of what it means to meditate, you may decide you would rather lie on your favorite rug and listen to bowling or whale sounds, or perhaps some soothing music. In this case the sounds of bowling balls crashing into pins, the howl of the whales, or the music will be our focus, taking the place of following our breath. The effect is the same: we let our minds go with the rhythm, pulling us wordlessly into another way of thinking. Meditation is our antidote to overthinking things. Lie still, let the sound wash over you, and listen for the silence within the noise. When Dudeism founder Oliver Benjamin appeared on ABC's Nightline program, he explained it like this: "Look at your mind like it's a radio, only instead of trying to find the station, you're trying to find the static."

We don't have to sit still – we can enter meditative states while in motion. Believe it or not, some people meditate best while doing routine actives, such as washing the dishes. Something most people find as a chore can become a serene experience when they use it as a moment to slow down and take joy in just being. The well-learned movements of such activity can act in the same way as our breathing does: It has a rhythm that we can follow and it requires no spoken words to complete. Like listening to whale song while gently allowing our bodies to move freely without preordained order, we can let our fears and emotions recede, replaced by a sense of being present.

Follow these steps if you are looking to add meditation to your life. You now have some incomplete instruction in meditation techniques. If this has sparked an interest move on to other sources of meditation instruction. Read other sources, find a teacher, or even join a meditation class. The addition of meditation can improve the quality of our abiding relationship with ourselves and the world at large.

How to Manage Money

The first thing to consider is what money means from the Dudeist perspective. Almost all of us must have some money to afford the basics in life. Beyond that, money can either be a source of joy or anguish. In Dudeism we look at how we earn money, and what we do with it to discern if it is truly making us happier.

Unless you are the heir to some mysterious fortune, you will have to earn some money to get by in this world. Remembering our Abiding Pyramid: it takes money, generally, to fulfill our physiological needs. Even the Dudeist must eat and pay their rent, hopefully before the tenth. If you can make it as a beach bum crashing on friends' couches, far out. However, there is nothing in Dudeism that says you cannot have a job to pay the bills, or even a career that can pay for a bit more than that.

For many, accumulating a vast fortune is the goal in itself, this is not so for the Dudeist. While the Dudeist may find themselves moving up into a higher tax bracket, that is not their focus. Ideally, the Dudeist may find riches through fulfilling their purpose.

Money is a tool we use to affect positive change in our lives, not an end goal in and of itself. Whether it is four, maybe five dollars, or a fortune, viewing money as secondary to other considerations is in line with Dudeist philosophy. Some people may become attached to their money, but the Dudeist should avoid this. As in any relationship, we seek to connect with money, while not letting it become something we pursue in disregard to the harm it may cause us.

As Dudeists, we look for ways to earn money through ethical and purposeful means. Take some time to consider what you would find to be satisfying work, then try to get paid for it. If you like to cook, maybe a career in in the food service industry is for you. If you enjoy reading about the philosophy and application of law, become a lawyer. What you do is less important than how it makes you feel when you do it. Noted Dudeist sage Epicurus advised that you find the right job for you, not the one that will fatten up your wallet the most. Find ways to fill your life with purpose, and the money will find a way to fill your bank account as well.

Spending money wisely is as important as how you earn it. It is best to only spend your clams on things that truly make you happy, and not only for a brief flashing moment. Carefully weighing all the aspects of a purchase based on the amount of happiness and harm it may cause. Not everything for sale will make you happy, despite what the ads or your daydreams may claim.

For instance, say you want a boat, but will owning one actually make you happier? Like a lot of things, a big ol' yacht looks like something fun to have, but there are many costs and responsibilities that may degrade any happiness it can provide. The bigger the boat, the bigger the headaches and fees. You may be able to afford a big boat, but can you afford the slip fees, the storage fees, maintenance, and fuel to use it? Suddenly finding yourself in debt to keep a boat may be a real bummer. Looking past our initial desires to see the bigger picture can save a lot of suffering. Not everything is right for everyone to own. Maybe you can afford the other costs and they are worth it to you, that is fine, you do you. What we are saying is to take a deep look at what it will be like to be in that situation before you get there.

That example can be applied to other ways we spend our money. Gambling can be fun, or it can be unhealthy. Having pets can make life feel fuller, or they can be a responsibility we are not ready for. The idea is to think about what will make you happy, and what will be a burden you are not really willing to carry.

So, now we have spent a little time discussing what money means within Dudeist philosophy, let us now talk about what to do with it if you have a few bucks kicking around. Good money management can save you a lot of troubles. Here are some tips for taking care of your finances and avoid headaches along the way.

- Balance your checkbook. Keep track of every transaction you make, even if it is just sixty-nine cents for a carton of half and half. Knowing how much you still have in your account before writing a bad check or scheduled withdrawal is the first step to avoiding fees and managing your money.

- Follow the money. Keeping track of where and how you spend your money is one of the best ways to eliminate unnecessary expenditures. There are fancy apps available online, but this can be accomplished with a pencil and a piece of paper, just like your grandaddy did it.

- Lay out a budget for yourself. Once you have followed the money find ways to trim costs for things that do not make your life better. This may leave you with more money to rent shoes at the bowling alley. Be sure to keep it realistic, do not try and cut things you really need or that give you a lot of happiness. Look for wasteful expenses that do not generate joy in your life and cut there.

- Stash your cash for a rainy day. Building up a savings account for unforeseen expenses, like needing rug cleaning services, can save one from having to borrow money when troubles happen. Even small contributions over time can add up to having enough on hand in the case of emergencies or other trying times.

- Avoid letting it become the tenth before paying your bills. Staying current with your normal expenses can help avoid a situation where debt begins to spiral out of control.

- Avoid and eliminate reoccurring charges that do not or no longer provide value through enriching your life. Maybe you signed up for a streaming service because they had *The Big Lebowski* available to watch, but now they dropped the best movie of all time, and you no longer use their service. Cut the cord, let that service go, man. Try to only keep reoccurring accounts that provide you with enjoyment worth their cost.

- Consider investing. You have followed these steps and now you have some extra money hanging around. Do some research and possibly invest those extra bones in a retirement account, the stocks, or your buddy's security business. Be careful and do your due diligence, only risk what you can afford, and try to only invest in things that are ethical and not harmful to others (or yourself).

We hope this incomplete financial guide has inspired you to better handle that check for being the handoff guy in a kidnapping plot. These are just the basics, but may they serve you well as you move into a higher tax bracket.

Rolling a J

Go ahead, we won't mind

Perhaps you have run a nice warm bath and got your rubber ducky ready, but something is still missing. Suddenly, you realize you need a J to go along with your relaxing soak. Here is how to twist up a joint that you will be proud to smoke, alone or with friends.

Cannabis has been utilized by humans for tens of thousands of years, if not longer. Commonly referred to as marijuana, ganja, and weed, cannabis is a wonder plant, with useful fibers for making cloth, rope and other items, and psychotropic qualities when smoked or ingested. There have been samples of hemp rope discovered that date back nearly 30,000 years. There has also been an archaeological discovery of some kind bud in China that dates back 2,700 years. So, it is safe to say cannabis has been used quite extensively in human history.

Fibers and rope are great, but today we're here to talk about the psychotropic flowers from either the sativa or indica types of cannabis plant. More precisely, we are going to give simple instruction to roll that sticky icky up in a J so it can be enjoyed.

Here is what you are going to need. Grab your favorite strain of weed, or whatever you have on hand; a means for breaking down those nuggs, such as a grinder or pair of scissors, you can use just your fingers if that is what you're into; rolling paper – there all sorts of options available, even flavored, but a standard 1.25 paper will serve you well. Then all you need is a few minutes and some patience to twist the bad boy up. You'll be doin' a J before you know it.

- First step it to break up the cannabis so that it burns nice and even like. Most buds will crumble easily if they have been properly cured. A grinder is the best way to go if you have one but chopping it up with scissors or your fingernails will work. You want the weed to be broken down small enough as to not be too chunky in the joint, but not so fine that it is powdery and spilling out the ends.
- Take your chosen paper and fold the bottom edge up to about the halfway point. Keep the glued part up and pointed in toward your fold. It helps if you pouch the ends by gently pushing them in to make a pocket to keep all that skunky goodness from falling out as you proceed.
- Start spreading the broken up weed evenly in the pouch. Poke it down with your finger to ensure it is not lumpy or all bunched up in one spot.
- Next, place your fingers over the doobage to keep it from spilling as you start rolling it up with your thumbs. This is the tricky part, take your time and enjoy the process, be artistic, this is not the time to get uptight.
- Pinch the whole assembly, and start rolling it back and forth to get it just tight enough, not too much, but if it is too loose you'll have an uneven burn.
- Once you have fussed over it to the point that it is looking good, give it the final roll up to the glued edge. Lick the glue and twist it all up.
- Check your work, take pride in the effort you put in. You can use a paperclip, pen, or other pointy object to poke any weed sticking out back into the

ends and twist them up to contain all that wonderful Mary Jane.

There you have it, one spiffy spliff. Kick back and do a J, we won't mind. You earned it.

It may be beneficial to note how it takes a certain patience to form the perfect jibber. Try to take the lessons learned from patiently investing time into rolling a splendid spliff into your daily life.

Mixing a White Russian

Careful, man, there's a beverage here

So now that you are feeling nice and limber after a relaxing bath and doing a J. Time to mix up a delicious drink and practice your yoga.

The White Russian is a classic drink, and enjoyed by not just a few Dudeists. Competently mixing a White Russian is a skill we feel is important for any Dudeist to know. Even if do not partake, being able to offer your guest a cold refreshing drink is a life skill that should be in your toolkit. Do not worry, it is not complicated, we aren't building the railroads here.

The White Russian was first concocted in the mid-60s. Far out, man. It is a variant of the Black Russian, so named because of the dark coffee liqueur and vodka that make up the cocktail. Thus, the addition of cream turns the drink into a White Russian, or Caucasian, if you prefer. Note that the reason the Dude calls a White Russian a Caucasian in the movie has nothing to do with skin color – the Caucasus mountains run through Russia.

You will need a rocks glass, some ice, a coffee liqueur such as Kahlua, vodka, and heavy cream (be sure to give it the smell test).

- Add ice to a rocks glass.
- Pour in 1 oz. of vodka.
- Add a half oz. of coffee liqueur.
- Stir.
- Top with a half oz. of heavy cream.

The ratio of ingredients can be altered if desired, and whether to stir in the cream is also a matter of taste. However, this basic recipe should be a good starting point if you are looking for a tasty beverage that even the Dude himself would dig.

Learning to pour just the right amount of just the right ingredients is one of the secrets to happiness, not just for a tasty libation. Like mixing a cocktail, life is about what we include in the mix, and using the right proportions for everything.

Cleaning a Pee-Stained Rug

They peed on your rug, Dude.

So, either some goons broke in and peed on your rug, or maybe just a pet was less than discreet when it came to where they relieved themselves. Getting peed on is one of the biggest risks that rugs face in their effort to tie a room together. This is how to clean up that offending liquid without getting caught up in a fake kidnapping caper.

Perhaps the easiest way to deal with a pee-stained rug is to call a professional if you have the clams for that sort of thing. A quick trip to the cleaner can help you avoid uncomfortable conversations with human paraquats or entanglements with heiresses whose art has been commended as being strongly vaginal. While the word vagina is not threatening to a Dudeist, artistic heiresses are well known robe thieves.

But, it's already the tenth and the landlord is looking for the rent. You have not recently moved up to a higher tax bracket, but you do have some basic cleaning supplies on hand. Well, the good news is that you can get rid of that stain, probably, all without having to make your buddy drive on Shabbos.

- If Woo just left and the stain is still wet, grab a cotton rag or paper towels to soak up any standing urine. Preventing urine from infiltrating the fibers of the rug is the best way to avoid staining. You can even use a shop-vac if you have one handy.
- Mix up a solution of 50% water and 50% white vinegar. Make sure to make enough of this

concoction to be useful. You can use a spray bottle to help saturate the area to be cleaned, or just slowly pour the solution on the stain. You may want to test the solution on an inconspicuous spot, to make sure you won't ruin the rug. Feel free to look up other home-made cleaning solutions to remove pee stains. This is just a basic recipe, but it should work in most cases.

- After you have applied the vinegar and water solution set about to scrubbing. It may sound exhausting, but vigorously using a quality scrub brush to remove the stain is your best bet here.
- Once you have scrubbed, taken a J break, and scrubbed some more, blot up the solution as thoroughly as possible and allow to dry.
- Almost there! Now you can sprinkle some baking soda on the area and vacuum it all up. This should leave most rugs stain-free and not smelling like Jackie's goons drug test.

If this did not work for you, time to call in the big guns – professional rug cleaners. They may even come to your home to take care of the issue without you having to wait for a team of investigators to find your car.

This should help any Dude to get his rug back to pristine condition. Because it really tied the room together, did it not?

THE INCOMPLETE DUDEIST PRIEST'S HANDBOOK

Shitting in the Woods

Does the Pope shit in the woods?

You bet he does. Humans have been pooping in the woods for longer than history can say, it is natural, and some may consider it a way of communing with nature. That said, there are rules to pooping in the wilderness, even in 'Nam.

So, you found yourself in the woods, out and about in nature when nature calls. Here is some handy information to have if you are camping, hiking, or hiding in the forest from nihilists. Whether you are taking a few days to cross the desert on a nameless horse or just chilling by the campfire, at some point you will have to go. It is incumbent on you to be in the know on how to go without polluting or leaving landmines for other wilderness visitors. It is every dude's job to protect the environment from their diet of cheeseburgers and white Russians. Don't pollute with your poop.

Human feces is a nuance and a biohazard when not handled properly. No Dudeist wants to be responsible for spoiling the health and beauty of natural spaces, so familiarizing yourself with proper procedures for shitting in the woods should be part of your preparations for any outdoor adventure.

Location, location, location. Knowing where not to leave your deposit is the first thing to consider. The general rule of thumb is to go at least a couple hundred feet from your camp and not on any trails.

The same applies to rivers, lakes, and streams. Walter does not need to see your turd barge floating by as he tries to wash his whites in the river. A sandy beach may seem like an easy place to dig a hole for you to use, but it is actually a terrible idea. Kids like to dig in the soft sand on the beach. Think of the children, man. Pooping far from any water source prevents the chances of you spreading disease and keeps the waterways in their unspoiled natural state.

Make sure you have the right equipment, such as a trowel or the means to pack your waste out with you when necessary. It will take more than a roll of biodegradable toilet paper to responsibly take care of your business while exploring any wild space.

Digging a Cathole

Digging a cathole is one of the oldest and simplest methods for pooping in the woods. Firstly, you do not want any foul orders interrupting the laughter around the campsite, so try and go at least two hundred feet, or about seventy paces from any campsite. Spread out the locations of cat holes if you plan to stay a while or if there is a group of people in the same area.

- Find a spot off the trails and away from campsites or sources of water. Look for easily dug loamy soil. Dig a hole at least six inches deep, but do not go deeper than the organic layer, as this will expedite your excretion's decomposition. In some desert locations the hole may be shallower, so check local recommendations in these circumstances if you can. Make the hole just big enough to be used without falling in or missing your target. About eight inches across.

- Once your cathole is ready, cop a squat and make like the Pope. If you are not planning to pack out your used toilet paper be sure to use a good camping tissue meant to break down faster than household types. If you are taking the used toilet paper out with you place it in a decent zip lock bag. This is not the time to be cheap, you do not want the bag busting open in your gear.

- Fill the hole back in and cover with leaves or other natural debris, mark with a stick in the ground if you are with a group or going to be in the same area for an extended time. This will prevent people from making a ghastly discovery when they go to dig their own cathole.

- Wash them hands. Use hand sanitizer when fresh water is not available, or every time, you can't play it too safe with the poo.

-

Digging a Latrine

A latrine is a good option when you are with a group of campers, you plan an extended stay in one spot, or you have small children with you. It can accommodate many uses and ensures that children who cannot dig their own catholes will be able to go without crossing the line.

The procedure for making a latrine is like the cathole as far as placement goes. The main difference is that they are a long trench instead of a singular hole in the ground. This allows multiple uses without having to dig individual holes for repeated use. Dig once, backfill as you go.

- Leave the excavated material on one side so that after each use the dirt can be easily thrown into the trench to cover up the offending deposit.
- Starting from one end do your business, then back fill that section. Continue to use the latrine, as you would a cathole. Use the latrine from one side to the other until you intend to leave the area, or the latrine has been completely filled.
- When finished with the latrine, cover with leaves or other natural camouflage, and mark with a stick or other means of remembering where you have already dug a latrine.
- Clean your hands with soap and water or sanitizer.

Take it With You

Leave no trace, that is the modern sensibility when it comes to venturing into natural areas. Many parks have made it a rule that human waste must not be left behind and should be deposited in the trash. This may mean you will have to carry out your waste with you.

"Eww!" is most people's first reaction, followed by a certain acceptance and then pondering the how of it all. Well, there's ways to manage this with some grace and decorum.

Bagging it up is a straightforward procedure, almost as easy as putting your bowling ball away. There are special bags available called WAG (Waste Alleviation and Gelling) bags. They lock in odor and aid in decomposition. They are easy to use, but here are a few things to remember.

- Pull your pants down. We should not have to mention this, but just in case you have walked in on the middle of the handbook.

- Squat and hold the edges of the bag, placement is key here.
- Use some biodegradable camping tissue and toss that in the bag as well.
- Close the bag and store in a separate strong bag to avoid any breakage or leaks.
- Then wash your hands and/or make like Saddam Hussein in the Dude's dream sequence with the disinfectant.

One tried and true method is the bucket toilet. There are commercial bucket toilets available, but they are a simple device made with a five-gallon bucket and some sort of seat for comfort and ease of use. With a commercial product simply follow the manufacturer's instruction. If you are constructing your own, here are some tips for using a bucket toilet.

- Same rules for placement, closer than two hundred feet from camp is over the line.
- Use a good biodegradable plastic bag to line your bucket.
- Choose a good biodegradable toilet paper, you should know this by now.
- Wash and/or sanitize those hands. Don't make us tell you again.
- Using a gelling powder will neutralize odors, solidify liquids, and begin breaking down solids. This is highly recommended.

One of the pros of using the five-gallon bucket plan is that you can jazz up you poo spot. Hang a tarp so that any rain will not ruin your communion with nature. Set up a tent around your loo to have privacy from any pervy wayward bears. Really go all out, make it nice. Hell, if you ain't married you can even leave the seat up.

Finally, there is the portable camp toilet. But, c'mon, man. If you are bringing your own fancy toilet, are you even camping? Just get a room at the Howard Johnson's and call it a day. We were going to go into more detail here but decided to go bowling instead. Just follow the instructions on the box. You got this.

The information above should aid any Dudeist who finds him or herself in need of relief in the wilderness. There is always more to know, so contact any park ranger for more information about going while going into the woods.

One thing a Dudeist can take away from these instructions is that as the old adage goes – "location, location, location." Paying attention to where your shit is, can be quite useful in life. It may save you from having to ask where your car is or inform you where your comfort zones are.

Avoiding and Surviving a Bear Encounter

Few people want to eat a bear, and even fewer want to be eaten by one. So, how do we avoid becoming a bear's mid-afternoon snack? The best way to avoid being Yogi's picnic basket is to not be where bears are. But perhaps you have wandered into the woods, dug your cathole, and now a bear has shown up to help you fill that hole with great haste. Here are some important tips to help you live to tell of the day you came face-to-face with a bear.

This is a good place to reiterate that this is an incomplete handbook. While we feel these tips are essential for anyone entering bear country, it is extremely important to be as informed as possible. Consult with park rangers, read up on the topic from reputable sources. Planning and knowledge are key to avoiding being a bear's meal.

Location, location, location

Bear attacks are not that common, but when they happen it can of course be devasting. As more people chose to live in and visit rural and natural areas, bear attacks have been rising. Knowing where bears frequent is the first step. If you are going to be camping know what type of bears may be in the region. Your first line of defense is knowledge about what species of bear you may encounter.

In North America there are three types of bears you may encounter: the black bear, the grizzly bear, and the polar bear. Knowing the habits and temperament of each type is important.

The most common is the black bear. They range throughout most of the northern part of the continent but are not limited to that area. They are the least of your worries, but still a formidable enemy should you encounter one in the wrong way. Typically, they have no interest in eating you, but they can be dangerous if startled or while protecting their young.

Probably the greatest threat is the grizzly bear. They are big and mean. It's best to stay out of their way entirely. While they have been known to be predatory towards humans, that is rare. Most attacks occur when they perceive humans as a threat. They will attack if they think you are after them, their cubs, or their food. They are far more commonly found in areas that humans frequent than the polar bear, so they pose a bigger threat in general, but polar bears are worse.

Polar bears are no fun. Overly aggressive, powerful, they will happily eat you. It is only because of their limited interactions with humans that they are not the biggest threat. Otherwise, they are the worst of the bunch when it comes to an encounter. They have been known to stalk and prey on humans. Our advice is to avoid them at all costs. If you are going to be where they are, this may be the only time we suggest borrowing Walter's gun. They are that bad.

Preparing for excursions into bear country is the first on the list.

- Find out what types of bears are going to be in any area you intend to visit. Learn to tell the difference between them, this helps in knowing how to react during an encounter.

- Have a plan for storing food. Bears love food, if you have the smell of it in your camp, they consider it an invitation.
- Carry bear spray or other defensive measures. Familiarize yourself on how to use bear spray, then visit Sobchak security and grab a can or two.

If we have not talked you out of that hike or camping trip, then here are somethings you can do to avoid seeing a bear altogether.

- Let them have the chance to avoid you. Bears generally do not want anything to do with humans. One of the biggest causes of a bear encounter are when you and the bear stumble upon each other. Make some noise to let them know you are there. If you're alone, talk to yourself. It's not weird in this case. Hiking in groups is also a good way to avoid bears. Be sure to talk or sing. Tell a joke! A few laughs just might save you from serious injury or worse.
- Be aware. Lookout for signs of bears such as tracks or piles of poo (technically called "scat"). Avoiding obvious feeding areas like patches of berries or sources of water where bears fish and drink.
- They may be good burgers you've brought, but do not keep them with you. Bears following the scent of food is a common cause of bear encounters. If you are camping put some distance between you and where you store your food. You can hang your food in a tree. It is recommended that the food be hanging 14 feet above the ground, 4 feet from the trunk of the tree, and around 100 yards from your camp. Try to achieve these suggestions whenever possible. Do not leave dirty plates, leftovers, or

wrappers in your camp, even these can attract bears who have an incredible sense of smell.

- Set up camp in an area where you have a lot of visibility. This ain't Nam, so avoid camouflaging your tent. You want to be able to see a bear coming, and you want them to see you. You're not hiding from men in black pajamas. You want to be seen.

Following those tips may help you avoid bears, but what do you do when you do see a bear? If the bear is fairly far away from you, good news, you can still avoid being lunch.

- Back away, but do not turn your back to the bear and run. Back up until you are out of sight, then put a few hundred yards between you and the bear.
- Take another route when possible.
- If you must go down the trail that you just saw the bear on, wait for a bit, 20 to 30 minutes at least. Then when you do continue down the trail make a bunch of noise. Give that bear every opportunity to know you are in the area, and for them to move on with their day of berry-picking.

What if it's too late? Either you neglected to follow our advice, or a bear has found you before you had a chance to let him know you're there. Now you are face to face with a bear and too close for comfort. This is the time that knowing which species of bear matters most.

If you are dealing with a black bear, you have a good chance of convincing them to just go away.

- If you come across a black bear while walking, stop and watch the bear to assess what its intent may be.
- If the bear does not make any moves toward you just start to back away slowly. Do not turn and run.

Never run from a bear. They are faster and that may initiate a predatory chase instinct.

- If the black bear starts to approach you, don't take that shit. Stand your ground and tell him to get lost. Do not yell in a panicked shriek, that may confuse and frighten them. Rather, be stern, like they are a bad dog you want off your lawn.
- Make yourself look big, puff up your chest and do not be a shrinking violet. Channel your inner Walter.
- If the black bear has entered your camp, inform them in a confident way that this is a private residence, man. Let them have an unobstructed path of escape. Have your bear spray at the ready or wield a big stick. Do not go on the offensive here. You just want them to know you are trouble if they give you any more grief. Let them know any aggression will not stand.

Shit! That's a grizzly. Grizzly bears make black bears look like Donny compared to Walter. You are not going to intimidate them into leaving you alone like you can with a black bear.

- Stand still and pay attention to what they do. Do not take your eyes off them. Again, never turn your back or run from a bear, we cannot stress this enough.
- Do not attempt to scare them off like a black bear.
- If they do not come at you, slowly back away while keeping an eye on them.
- If they start to approach you, this is the time to use that bear spray that we told you to pack, and hope it works.

In the case of polar bears, just don't. Do not go where they are, and if you must, yeah, bring a gun. No bullet-point list is a match for a real bullet in this case. Polar bears are far too dangerous, thankfully they are in areas that most people will never go. Polar bears make grizzlies look downright reasonable, so it's best to avoid them.

You have done all the right things to avoid encountering a bear, but it just has not worked in your favor. Despite using bear spray and your best efforts to avoid or dissuade them, that bear is coming for you and an attack is imminent. The question of whether to remain a pacifist or to tell them bear they're in for a world of hurt depends on why the bear is attacking. There are two reasons a bear attacks, defensive or predatory, and knowing the difference and how to respond is a matter of life and death in this instance. In either case, never run from a bear, especially when it is in attack mode.

Defensive attacks are a case of the bear feeling threatened or protecting its young, these are the most common. The bear will do things like make a false charge at you, take little hops in your direction, huff and puff, clack and show its teeth, or slap the ground. This is how a bear says across this line you do not. The bear may not commit to its attack, if so, slowly back away while keeping eye contact, you lucky bastard. If the bear does attack, here are the steps to take to possibly survive the encounter.

- Play dead.
- Lock your fingers together behind your neck. This will protect the sensitive area that bears like to go for.
- Lay flat on your stomach with your elbows and legs spread out to make it harder to roll you over. Or-
- Curl up in the fetal position to endure the assault.

- Once the attack ends stay still and do not move for at least twenty to thirty minutes. Give the bear plenty of time to move along and leave you be.

If you are the target of a predatory attack from a bear, channel your inner Walter and fight back as if your life depends on it. Because it does. This is absolutely not the time to hide behind your pacifism, be as aggressive as possible. Use any weapon at your disposal. Grab a rock or big club from the surroundings if you must. Aim for the sensitive parts of the face, the nose, and eyes. Continue to fight back hard until the bear decides you are not worth the trouble, hopefully.

We sincerely wish that you never have to use any of these tips for not being eaten by a bear. However, if you do, we hope you are successful and can come back to Dudeism's little beach community with a wild tale to tell. Good luck out there, Dudes.

It is noteworthy to mention that these techniques can also be applied to encounters with less furry aggressors. Avoiding threatening nihilists or other toxic individuals when you can, backing out of uncomfortable or dangerous situations can be a good way out of a bad situation, sometimes. When avoidance or backing away is not working, knowing when to not hide behind your pacifism and stand your ground may save you from unchecked aggression or undudeness in the long run. Take some time to recognize what you are dealing with, not just with bears, but for all the things that come and go in life.

Finding a D&D Game

You have survived soiled rugs, shitting in the woods, and even avoided being eaten by a bear. Now all you want to do is have a few laughs with your friends, but they have closed the local bowling. What's a Dude to do?

Play is an important part of maintaining an abiding lifestyle and bowling has the affection of many a Dudeist. However, it is getting harder and harder to find a bowling alley these days, and sometimes it is difficult to make the trek to the ones that are still open. So, we looked around for an activity that might be more accessible, and still focused on commadore and friendship building. That is when we stumbled across Dungeons and Dragons.

No longer the presumed Satan-worshipping ire of church ladies across the nation, D&D has seen a resurgence in popularity over the last few years. More and more people are playing D&D than ever. The game has even become a spectator sport with the success of web series such as Critical Role and High Rollers attracting millions of viewers. There are even games played in auditoriums full of screaming fans. Remember, just as what happened with superheroes and computers, what was once nerdy and weird usually becomes cool and mainstream at some point.

Role-playing games like D&D have a lot to offer the modern Dudeist. For one thing, a lot of them are now played online, meaning you can easily play in your favorite bathrobe without having to leave your comfy abode. Games like this are cooperative, not competitive, there is no need to trash talk or pull a gun on the lanes. They tend to build or strengthen lasting friendships through the unfolding of a unique shared experience.

Online or in person, roleplaying games allow the Dudeist to go on crazy adventures and deal with zany characters, just like the Dude. There are mysteries to solve, kidnap victims to rescue, and powerful beings to call paraquats. If your friend dies in the final battle against a bunch of nihilists you can mourn that character, then reroll a new one. A character's funeral in game you won't even leave you covered in their ashes.

If you are interested in D&D or other roleplaying games first ask, how do you want to do this? Online or in person?

If you want to play in person start by asking your friends if they are into that sort of thing. The best games start with a group of players who already know each other. If none of your friends are into the whole dungeon crawling thing, your next best bet is to find your local gaming store. They sometimes have game nights that you can jump right into, or information about games looking for players. Not very exhausting, sounds easy.

Finding an online game is even easier than that. You can simply type into your browser "looking for D&D game." There are subreddits, Facebook groups, Roll20, and a bevy of other resources for hooking up with a chill bunch of people to face down epic villains with.

In either case you will want to have a good idea of what your available time to play is, and what sort of play style you are looking for. There is almost always a game that fits your schedule, and plenty that lean into either roleplay or combat to choose from.

All that is left is to just kick back, mix a White Russian, and join in the fun.

The advice here does not exclusively apply to finding some like-minded role-playing compeers. Look for activities that can inspire you that you can share with others. Remember, the true achievement is building friendships and camaraderie, not the slaying of dragons or rolling the perfect game.

How to Take a Slacker Nap

You have been through a lot in this life skills section, everything from cleaning rugs and finding games to avoiding becoming a bear's dinner. You must be wiped out! Well, it's time for a nap, then. An afternoon nap holds many benefits for both mental and physical health. Many successful people find that naps add to their overall productivity. We will leave so-called "power-napping" to the overachievers, but any Dudeist could also reap the rewards of the occasional slacker nap.

Many people feel the urge to lie down and chill in the afternoon. It can be a rewarding and enjoyable experience and also allow you to regather your vigor. While naps can help refresh your energy levels during the mid-day slump, they are also good for your health. Medical science suggests that naps can boost a person's immune system, protecting them against viruses and other ailments. The trick is, how to make the most of your naptime? *The Incomplete Dudeist Priest's Handbook* is here with some useful tips for getting the most out of doing the least.

- When to nap? Early afternoon might be best. Sometime between 1 and 3 p.m. is generally a good time for most people to take a nap. That's about the time most people start to feel tired during the day. Taking a nap much later may interfere with your regular sleep time.
- Finding the right place to nap is also essential. While one's bed may be good for some, it may cause others to sleep too long, leaving them groggy from

a nap intended as a recharge. A couch or comfy chair are other good options.

- A good length of time for a slacker nap is about 20-30 minutes. That's enough time to feel rested, without falling into a deep sleep and possibly finding yourself still tired or upsetting regular sleep patterns.
- You can stay and finish your coffee. In fact, people report that drinking a cup of coffee right before lying down for a nap helps them not fall too deeply into slumber, and they wake up refreshed with a caffeine jolt to help restart their productivity, if you're into that sort of thing.

Many cultures have incorporated an afternoon nap into their daily lives, and so too can Dudeists. If you have the opportunity and you are feeling a little tuckered out in the afternoon it may be time for a slacker nap. Lie down and recharge those batteries, who knows, maybe you have a league game coming up, and you want to roll your best. Arriving at the lanes tired is not going to help your team get into the finals. So, kick back and let that siesta do its thing.

Napping also reminds us to pay attention to our bodies and minds, allowing for time to reset when we feel overwhelmed or exhausted. As you plan for your slacker nap, think about other ways you might want to slow things down, and let yourself relax when you need it.

Dudeist Prayers

Here are some Dudeist prayers. Although they're more poetic and fun than an appeal to anything serious and metaphysical, they can still have a moving, almost spiritual effect on our mindset. Use them as you see fit: as inspiration, a daily mantra, or as readings for Dudeist ceremonies. Dudeist prayers are meant to capture the intent of Dudeism in a way that can be shared among all Dudeists, so repeat them with the understanding that you are not alone, Dude.

The Dude's Prayer
(Based on the Lord's Prayer)

Our Dude, who art in Los Angeles,

Hallowed be thy handle.

Thy rug will come.

Thy chill be done

All over Earth, as it is in your bungalow.

Give us this day our daily caucasian,

And forgive us our stresspasses,

As we forgive those who stresspass against us.

And lead us not into Simi Valley,

But deliver us from real reactionaries and human paraquat.

For thine is the lane, and the ball, and the what-have-you,

Down through the ages, across the sands of time.

Fuckin' A man.

— *By Rev. John Jansson*

The Calm Psalm
A.K.A. The Dude is my Brother Shamus
(based on Psalm 23)

Psalm 23 of the Christian Bible is one of the most popular passages, often repeated. It affirms one's faith that the universe is taking care of you. Dudeism has a similar attitude. In the passage below, "The Dude" is not a person, but a way of living, an attitude, and philosophy. If we follow the way of the Dude, our troubles are over, man.

The Dude is my Brother Shamus; I shall abide.

He helpeth me lay down on valued rugs.

He leadeth me into the bubblebath waters.

He bringeth new information to light.

Yea, though I walk through the seamy valleys, in the shadows of dipshits,

I will fear no Nihilists; for they are cowards.

Thou preparest a table for me with burgers, beers, a few laughs.

Thou refilleth my White Russian.

Careful man! My beverage runneth over.

Surely limberness shall follow me all the days of my life. Is this a – what day is this?

And I will abide in the Dude's Abode indefinitely.

Fuckin'A, man.

— *By Reverend Oliver Benjamin*

The Serendipity Prayer
(based on the Serenity Prayer)

Dude, grant me the ease to not be worried about all that shit,

the courage to say when this aggression will not stand,

and the wisdom to know the difference.

(do these go together?)

Living one day at a time,

Enjoying one moment at a time,

Accepting that new shit will always come to light;

Laughing at the whole durn human comedy,

Not trying to make it stop and start at my convenience;

Trusting that nothing is fucked here!

The plane has not crashed into the mountain!

Thus, you remind me to always abide today,

So that my thinking will never be uptight tomorrow.

Fuckin' A, man.

I Am The Walrus. (kinda seems like this is supposed to be the title?)

— By Reverend Dr. Charlie J. Perkins

Dudeist Affirmation

Dude, I shall abide with the things I cannot change,

Give a shit about the things I can change,

And not be a fucking moron who doesn't know the difference.

— By Reverend Gary M. Silvia

A Dudeist's Wish

May we abide as the Dude abides, with as little effort as possible.

May we cherish the ups in life, as if we were throwing strikes.

May we abide in the face of downers, as simply as ordering a beer.

May we find good friends to share our lives with, both special and otherwise.

May we find calm in this uptight world, as if we found our venue.

May we take comfort in this continuing human comedy, as a stranger would.

May we pass through this absurd existence unburdened, as a tumbleweed.

This is the Dudeist's wish, for one and all.

— *By Reverend Gary M. Silvia*

The Dudely Vow

As an ordained Dudeist priest, I (state your name) vow:

To just take it easy, man

To spread the Dude word when it's not too exhausting

To always make time to have some burgers, some beers, a few laughs

To always check in to see what condition my condition is in

To not treat objects like women, man

To keep my mind limber

To enjoy natural, zesty enterprises

And always, in a whole world gone crazy, to abide

Down through the generations, across the sands of time.

So help me Dude.

— By Reverends Oliver Benjamin and Dwayne Eutsey

Conclusion

Well, we hope you've found this handbook enlightening and informative. Maybe we even shared a few laughs along the way.

The goal of *The Incomplete Dudeist Priest's Handbook* is to prepare the Dudeist practitioner for some of the issues that may arise as they engage with the world. We have addressed philosophical questions. The purposes for and how to conduct Dudeist ceremonies. We have even given some basic life skills to aid the Dudeist in everyday situations, or some not so ordinary circumstances.

With this handbook you should now feel confident explaining to your friends what Dudeism is blathering about, you should know what Dudeism is and is not, and you should have some understanding of human needs and why we pursue them. We have provided our best explanation for what it means to abide and live as a Dudeist priest. Of course, as this handbook is incomplete, we will surely add more to it, down through the ages. Feel free to offer suggestions here: www.dudeism.com/idh.

Now that you are inspired, informed, and entertained, go on to be the sort of Dudeist priest we can all be proud of.

Bar's over there.

Made in the USA
Columbia, SC
21 November 2024

488536b9-d5a5-4b64-91a1-0e91f30b8bf8R01